THE MASS MARKETING OF POLITICS

*This book is dedicated to Judy Newman,
my wife and best friend.*

*Judy, thank you for your loving support
and for sharing in my excitement of politics.
This book is yours as much as it is mine.*

BRUCE I. NEWMAN

THE MASS MARKETING OF POLITICS

DEMOCRACY IN AN AGE OF MANUFACTURED IMAGES

SAGE Publications
International Educational and Professional Publisher
Thousand Oaks   London   New Delhi

For information:

 SAGE Publications, Inc.
2455 Teller Road
Thousand Oaks, California 91320
E-mail: order@sagepub.com

SAGE Publications Ltd.
6 Bonhill Street
London EC2A 4PU
United Kingdom

SAGE Publications India Pvt. Ltd.
M-32 Market
Greater Kailash I
New Delhi 110 048 India

Printed in the United States of America

Library of Congress Cataloging-in-Publication Data

Newman, Bruce I.
    The mass marketing of politics: Democracy in an age of manufactured images / by Bruce I. Newman.
        p.   cm.
    Includes bibliographical references and index.
    ISBN 0-7619-0958-3 (cloth: alk. paper)
    ISBN 0-7619-0959-1 (pbk.: alk. paper)
    1. Electioneering—United States.   2. Marketing—United States.
3. Presidents—United States—Election.   4. Democracy—United States.
5. United States—politics and government—20th century.   I. Title.
    JK2281 .N484   1999
    324.7'2'0973—dc21   99-6266

        00   01   02   03   04   05   7   6   5   4   3   2

Acquisition Editor:	Harry Briggs
Editorial Assistant:	MaryAnn Vail
Production Editor:	Astrid Virding
Editorial Assistant:	Patricia Zeman
Typesetter:	Lynn Miyata
Indexer:	Cristina Haley

Contents

Foreword

Why are so many voters turned off by today's political campaigns? Why do so few people take advantage of their precious right to vote? Why do so few citizens participate in politics? Is our democratic process at risk because of apathy and indifference?

These important questions are carefully analyzed in this thoughtful book by a respected scholar and marketing expert, Bruce I. Newman of DePaul University. Newman insightfully sums up his case as follows:

> Our electoral system originally was set up to give candidates the opportunity to let voters know who they are and what they stand for during the course of a primary campaign. However, an interesting twist has taken place in politics today. Through the use of scientific polling, candidates now use marketing research to do just the opposite, that is, to find out who the voters are and what they want the candidates to stand for. Candidates can then feed back to the voters the ideas that they know will sell in the marketplace. (p. 16)

What is new about this development is the astonishing sophistication of contemporary commercial marketing techniques that are now being used by professional political consultants. Primary elections originally were created by reformers who wanted to get rid of the old-fashioned cigar-smoking political bosses in the back room. What happened is that we replaced the old bosses with new bosses, described by Newman as political consultants who are now the "coaches and managers who determine the outcome, with the media serving as umpires" (p. 18). So, although we might have gotten rid of the old smoke-filled room, the new smoke-free room is occupied by a new breed of bosses who know how to manipulate new marketing techniques to influence voters.

The power of the new consultants extends beyond campaign periods. Consultants remain after the election. Their advice eliminates the difference between campaigning and governing. When a candidate wins an election, he or she brings into office the same consultants who helped win the victory, and the same process continues on.

A major cause of the problem is our method of campaign finance. Former Senator Paul Simon believes that citizens are wrong when they think that Congress is an unresponsive institution. To the contrary, both Simon and Newman think that Congress is excessively responsive—to the polls and to campaign contributors. The problem, as they perceive it, is that this responsiveness (to the wrong people) is leading to the erosion of national leadership. I think that they are right. New and creative ideas about campaign finance are needed, including public service television time for candidates that is now provided in most other democracies. The British system works very well, and we could adopt it for our country.

This book is important because it casts new light on the future of campaigns, the future of elections, and the future of the democratic process. Today's cynicism about politics is dangerous for our political health and could be deadly for our children. We can govern ourselves wisely only if we have abundant, factual, relevant information about candidates' talent and character rather than their consultants' slick versions of what they think we want to see and hear. That is why *The Mass Marketing of Politics* deserves your thoughtful reading and reflection.

Newton N. Minow
Counsel, Sidley & Austin
Chicago
(Former chairman, Federal Communications Commission)

Preface

The Mass Marketing of Politics makes it very clear why our democracy is on shaky ground: Leaders in Washington, D.C., are completely disconnected from the American people. The impeachment of the president of the United States turned into a political campaign, with a reliance on partisanship over the will of the American people. When the Monica Lewinsky case broke in January 1998, the American people had a sitting president whose job approval ratings hovered close to 60%, even on the eve of his impeachment by the House of Representatives. To the amazement of political analysts, Bill Clinton has successfully manufactured two different images of himself: one as the president and one as a private citizen.[1] In fact, many people have questioned how the president has been able to keep the two images separate and distinct in the minds of so many people. The answer to that question lies in this book.

Mass marketing techniques that have made Coca-Cola a household name have been used by Clinton to communicate with the American people. The key difference is that the vast majority of Americans know Clinton only from the image they see of him on television. The White House knows this and has spent millions of dollars on polling and focus groups to monitor how people perceive the president's ideas. There are no limits to the use of polls in the modern presidency, including Clinton's use of this tool to monitor the mood of the nation before deciding that it was not in his best political interests to tell the American people the truth about his relationship with Lewinsky. The presidency has turned into a "permanent campaign," making reliance on mass marketing techniques inevitable and potentially dangerous to the health of our democracy.

The ideas expressed in this book move back and forth between the world of corporations and their products and the world of politicians and their ideas. The reader will find comparisons of the image manufacturing of successful companies such as Gatorade with the use of similar tactics by famous presidents such as Franklin D. Roosevelt. Just as Gatorade has relied on testimonials by basketball superstar Michael Jordan to convey a popular image of its product, Roosevelt tried to convey an image of resiliency by painting his steel braces black to camouflage them so that people could not tell that he was disabled. The book takes the reader behind the scenes in the White House to reveal how the Clinton marketing juggernaut has managed to reengineer the president's image in the face of one crisis after another.

The reader might be shocked to find out that there are not any restrictions on what a candidate can say in a political commercial. Whereas the Federal Trade Commission has jurisdiction over what McDonald's and other companies say in television commercials, they have no such power when it comes to political advertising. The response to this by politicians has been the excessive use of negative advertising, leaving the American electorate turned off by politics and distrustful of its leaders.

The same marketing mentality that drives political campaigns has spilled over into the running of government, with politicians and interest groups framing policy around multimillion-dollar advertising campaigns. The insurance industry won the health care debate with its "Harry and Louise" commercials, and the tobacco industry was equally successful in its national debate by bankrolling a $40 million advertising campaign. As the cost to drive public opinion and position ideas escalates in this country, more and more money will be needed to fuel the marketing campaigns that political parties and interest groups must run if they want to manufacture winning images. Without some type of political reforms, we as a country will find our democracy hopelessly spun into a web of influence that is out of the control of ordinary citizens.

My main motivation for writing this book is to help educate an American electorate that is very frustrated with the state of its political affairs and to offer an explanation behind the changes taking place. The state of our democracy is at a turning point, and I am convinced that informed citizens will be in a much better position to respond to the challenge our country faces. My hope is that the information conveyed in this book will help all of us to better understand what actions need to be taken to ensure that our democracy is strengthened in the future.

This book will be of particular interest to anyone who studies the American political system and wants to update his or her knowledge on advances taking place technologically and in the media. Politicians, consultants, pollsters, journalists, political party officials, and all the other people who are part of the political process in this country will find the book refreshingly candid about their influence on the system. Anyone who has given any thought to the possibility of an outsider—a virtual unknown—winning the U.S. presidency will want to read this book. Finally, a solution is put forward to the millions of Americans who would like to know how we can salvage a political system that seems bent on self-destruction.

Countless hours have been spent researching and writing this book over a 4-year period, but without the help of some key people, this book never would have been completed in a timely fashion. First, I thank my editor at Sage Publications, Harry Briggs, for being so receptive to the ideas I put forward to him about this book and for being supportive throughout the project. It continues to be a pleasure to work with him. I also thank all of the wonderful professionals at Sage who have been involved in the editing and production of my book, especially MaryAnn Vail, D. J. Peck, Astrid Virding, and Lisa Kamins Joy. Thank you for making Sage a company with which I continue to enjoy working.

In the very early stages of this book, Linda Bendixen, a former journalist and student of mine, was very helpful in her editing work. Another person who was very supportive in the early stages of this book was Rick Perloff, a professor of communication at Cleveland State University. His insights into the effects of persuasion on voters were extremely constructive. Another very helpful person early on was Lawrence Hamer, my colleague in the marketing department at DePaul University. He challenged some of the central ideas I put forward in the book and helped me to crystallize my thinking. Two other colleagues at DePaul, Nina Diamond and Doug Lamont, provided constructive comments on later drafts of the book. In particular, Nina was very instrumental in helping me to separate the role of marketing from that of advertising in politics and society. My research assistants, Brent Stewart, Melissa Rose and Elena O'Curry, helped with the tedious but important job of organizing the references used throughout the book. Also, I want to thank Robin Florzak of the media relations department at DePaul University for her insightful comments.

Finally, I thank some of my family members for their constant support and help during the long journey of writing this book. To Judy, my wife, thanks for all of the wonderful conversations we have had about the political issues I have raised in this book. Sometimes, I wonder whether I might have turned you, the artist, into a political junkie like me. To my dad, Samuel, thanks for always listening so patiently to me whenever I had ideas to share with you. To Todd, my son, thanks for never saying a word to me when I came to your baseball games with my manuscript in hand to edit as I sat and watched you play. To Erica, my daughter, who told me that she liked the fact that I am an author except when it took time away from going to the "blue park" with her to play tag, thanks for being so understanding. And to my nephew George, who just graduated from high school, thanks for your poignant insights into how the young people in this country think about politics.

NOTE

1. Manufacturing images in the mass media is discussed in Phillips, J. (n.d.). *The age of the infotoxin.* Available on Internet: http://www.adbusters.org/main/index.html.

Introduction

The date was November 3, 1992, and Bill Clinton was about to approach the stage at the governor's mansion to give his acceptance speech. The scene about to be described appears at the end of the documentary, *The War Room,* a movie that recounts the final days of the inside workings of the Clinton/Gore 1992 campaign organization. A jubilant George Stephanopolous is seen standing in the middle of a crowd of people, speaking to Clinton over a cellular telephone:[1]

> Governor . . . it's a landslide . . . it's unbelievable. . . . I'm the happiest man in the world, and I just got to tell ya, I really appreciate it. It's the best thing I ever did. We really want you to say whatever you want to say tonight, but you just have to be careful about being too programmatic. You definitely should be a New Democrat, and we love Hillary's new patriotism thing. . . . Speak from your heart tonight, I mean, that's all that matters. Say what you want to say, I mean, this is your night. We'll see you in a little bit. Bye-bye.

The final shot in the movie is of Clinton speaking to the crowd, saying, "And finally, I want to thank the members of my brilliant, aggressive, unconventional, but always winning campaign staff."

There is a lot of applause and laughter as well as shots of James Carville smiling ear to ear, and then Clinton says, "and they have earned this."

The "war room," and the mentality that it cultivated, lived on after Clinton entered the White House and has become the hi-tech factory where any information about the president is monitored and redisseminated to carefully craft and manufacture his image. Why do we live in an age where politicians have to manufacture their images? Because the vast majority of citizens in the United States never have the opportunity to meet their leaders and only get to know them through the images they see on television, read about in newspapers and magazines, and hear about on radio.

In this modern age of 24-hour news cycles and 30-second sound bites, unforgettable visual images can be frozen in time with a glance of the head or a bead of sweat. Let us not forget the infamous presidential debate in 1992 when George Bush looked down at his watch in a momentary fit of uneasiness, or the beads of sweat that slowly grew on Richard Nixon's upper lip as he debated John F. Kennedy in 1960. When an unforgettable visual image is matched with words equally remarkable in their tone and content, the image may become a fixture in the political psyche of a nation, as many believe will happen to a determined-looking Clinton wagging his finger at the camera in the White House saying, "I did not have sexual relations with that woman [Monica Lewinsky]."

Yes, the world has witnessed a significant political change during the 20th century, with nearly every country now participating in the democratic process of choosing its leaders. Momentous technological changes also have taken place in commerce during this past century, beginning with the invention of the automobile. Americans watched in amazement at the ability of Henry Ford to mass market his Model T Ford, making it affordable to the ordinary man or woman. The Model T was the first of many more products that would be mass marketed to the American people during the 20th century such as gym shoes, television sets, radios, and cameras—identical products all mass produced along assembly lines and distributed to millions of consumers.

Mass production techniques certainly were nothing new to Ford, who must have borrowed these same methods from manufacturers such as Colt, which assembled and sold guns on a mass scale. During the 19th century, manufacturers such as Colt were mass producing guns that used interchangeable parts. What separates the mass production techniques of the 19th century from the mass marketing techniques of the 20th century is the importance that has been placed on image manufacturing.

Take the Nike corporation, for example. Here we have a company run by Philip Knight, who through his marketing genius has steered Nike to the top of his industry, due in large part to the infamous "swoosh" symbol on all Nike products. The swoosh is a simple but highly recognizable trademark that identifies the Nike corporation and, at the same time, communicates a message of quality, success, and other positive emotions. Why? Because the most successful athletes in nearly every sport can be seen by millions of adoring fans wearing it on some parts of their uniforms. And the Nike story does not end here.

Knight's empire was shaken at its very core when it came to the public's attention that Nike was using people in Indonesia to manufacture its products. The story that came out in the mass media revealed that Nike was using underaged, underpaid workers who were working in horrible conditions. So, what did Knight do? He increased the minimum wage, limited the number of working hours, and increased the age requirements. Through technological improvements in his factories, he eliminated the amount of toxins released in the air in his factories. Furthermore, Knight became a human rights advocate and, in the process, worked to improve his company's image in the minds of millions of consumers who buy its products.

Nike is now one of the companies leading the fight on human rights abuses in the workplace and certainly has received its share of criticism. But one can only hope that this is the story of a company responding to the needs of its customers and the public in a positive and constructive manner. If that is the case, then this is an example of image manufacturing being used to build a better society. If not, this is marketing at its worse, where a company takes advantage of people in one country to broaden its market base in other countries.

As we enter the new millennium, the same mass marketing techniques used by corporations are being used to craft and deliver images of political leaders to citizens in democratic countries all over the world. Through the aid of television, computers, database technologies, and multimillion-dollar advertising campaigns, politicians are winning office and governing through the use of sophisticated marketing techniques that drive public opinion. The political system today is driven by marketing with an emphasis on image over substance, on personality over issues, on 30-second sound bites over meaningful dialogue, and on technological changes that have altered how information is communicated in the media. Political news has become entertainment in this country. News stations are run by corporations that have budgets and revenue goals to meet. It has become near impossible for politicians to get coverage of meaningful issues on the evening news. It seems that the viewing public would rather hear about the private sex lives of its leaders, or watch people get into fights on the *Jerry Springer* show, than listen to candidates debate the issues. Being the good marketers that they are, the major television networks have responded to the needs of their customers. Unfortunately, people's needs are shaped by the tremendous loss of respect for politicians in Washington, D.C., these days.

A disturbing portrait of the American electorate came out in the results of a study carried out by the Committee for the Study of the American Electorate, a nonpartisan organization, which concluded that the majority of eligible voters have simply given up on the election process. One statistic this group cites is that only 16.9% of eligible voters cast their ballots in the 1998 primaries, 48% lower than the previous record set in 1970. Curtis Gans, director of the study, states, "If there is something important to decide, citizens will come out and vote. . . . On the other hand, it is apparent that, in the majority of elections, citizens increasingly see little of importance to decide and are decreasingly

motivated either by partisan interest or civic duty." Gans goes on to say, "The
level of party participation has fallen so low that we are . . . threatening the
cohesion of American politics and in danger of one or another party being
captured by the fringes." The study further concludes that the declines in voting
are most pronounced among voters who are younger, less educated, and worse
off economically.[2]

Today, we are witnessing candidates and politicians going to almost any
length to win and hold onto office. The American people are becoming more
and more disillusioned with a political system that is for sale at any price, thus
cheapening their democracy. The danger to society is that the same consumers
who are used to product marketing are not paying close enough attention to the
politicians' use of these tactics. Unlike the commercial marketplace, where the
Federal Trade Commission can ban advertising that is deceptive, no such
guidelines exist for political commercials. In a Supreme Court ruling in 1976,
political communication was equated with free speech, thereby preventing the
government from regulating a candidate's commercials. What does this mean?
It means that a candidate can make any accusation about an opponent without
being held accountable.

What is further alarming about today's political system is the role that money
plays in the electoral process. For any candidate interested in competing in the
presidential primaries, a total of $20 million must be raised a full year before
the first primary takes place. This amounts to raising more than $50,000 a day
for a full year. Political campaigns have turned into full-blown marketing
campaigns. Campaign organizations are relying on the same technology that
has enabled universities to raise staggering amounts of donations in very short
periods of time. Using sophisticated computer databases that reveal its alumni's
relative wealth and inclinations to give money, Northwestern University raised
$457 million in only 1½ years.[3]

Multimillion-dollar advertising campaigns are not limited to politicians.
Today, lobbying arms of industries are targeting politicians with their issue
campaigns. The tobacco industry spent $40 million in its advertising campaign
to kill the Senate's antismoking legislation. Some senators thought that the
8-week advertising blitz that positioned the legislation as a "tax and spend" bill
helped play a role in killing the proposal. According to Alan Pilkington, president of DDB Needham Chicago (a large advertising firm), "People form their
opinions based on television. . . . It has turned into a very useful surgical tool."[4]

What has Congress done to put a stop to this alarming increase in money
being spent to fuel the marketing campaigns? Nothing. Not surprisingly, the
Democrats and Republicans have very different ideas on how to fix the system.
Even though the American public wants some type of campaign reform, efforts
by leaders in both parties have failed to materialize.

In the Senate, the McCain-Feingold campaign reform bill would have put a ban on so-called "soft money" contributions, namely those that are ostensibly for party-building activities but, in practice, often are used to pay for multi-million-dollar advertising campaigns that benefit targeted candidates in crucial races. The Democrats have charged that the soft money contributions have ignited a money chase that favors wealthy special interests over ordinary people. The Republicans, clearly more successful than the Democrats in raising this type of money, have claimed the opposite and argue that campaigns are underfunded. The Republicans point to the outdated reforms instituted during the 1970s that limit individual contributions to each candidate to $1,000. The Republicans want the limits raised and disclosure requirements stiffened to let people know where the candidates' money is coming from. This last idea is a great one, but if history is any guide, this would take so much time to follow through on that the election would be over by the time the disclosure was made public.[5]

During Franklin D. Roosevelt's time, most Americans knew what it meant to be a Democrat or a Republican, a liberal or a conservative, and Roosevelt's National Recovery Act was used to help him implement his working ideology. But today, the labels "liberal" and "conservative" in politics no longer are defined by the political parties; instead, they are defined by the candidates themselves and the images that their consultants craft for them. Clinton said early in his presidency that his ideas were neither liberal nor conservative but rather both.[6]

Politics today is waged in the media, from military invasions, to impeachment hearings, to issue campaigns. At the heart of each of these campaigns is the use of image manufacturing. Separating fact from fiction is becoming inherently more difficult for average citizens as they try to decipher the meaning of messages targeted to them by political action committees, politicians, talk radio personalities, and others. If our political system continues to move in its current direction, we run a great risk of making it possible for the wrong person to take control of our country.

So, what does determining public opinion have to do with true leadership? How healthy is it for a candidate to enter office solely on the basis of images carefully crafted in the media? Does society benefit when a president's ideology and actions are driven by marketing? Can a democratic government succeed when making public policy decisions that are driven by marketing goals? Finally, how has Clinton kept his approval ratings so high in the face of all the allegations leveled at him? The answers to these questions are examined in this book. The book shows how marketing has changed the very fabric of our democracy, points out the potential pitfalls of relying too heavily on marketing, and offers some solutions for fixing our political system before it is too late.

NOTES

1. *War Room.* Documentary film on the 1992 Clinton presidential campaign. Producers, Frazer Pennebaker, R. J. Cutler, and Wendy Ettinger. Executive producers, Frazer Pennebaker and Wendy Ettinger (1993). VHS Published/Distributed by Vidmark Entertainment (1994).

2. Tackett, M. (1998, June 19). A record low turnout possible in November. *Chicago Tribune,* sec. 1, p. 6.

3. Jones, P. M. (1998, May 31). Competition fuels colleges' megabucks fundraising. *Chicago Tribune,* sec. 1, p. 1.

4. Kirk, J. (1998, June 19). Tax-and-spend theme of ad blitz apparently hit home with senators. *Chicago Tribune,* sec. 1, p. 3.

5. CNN-Time. (1997, November 6). *In focus: Campaign reform.* Available on Internet: http://www.allpolitics.com.

6. Woodward, B. (1994). *The agenda: Inside the Clinton White House.* New York: Simon & Schuster.

The Impact of Marketing on Democracy

The people's government, made for the people, made by the people, and answerable to the people.

—Daniel Webster, second speech in the Senate
on Foote's Resolution, January 26, 1830

The presidency (and government) used to operate in a very predictable manner in this country. Candidates running for president used to build grassroots organizations of thousands of volunteers, who passed out leaflets about the candidates from door to door. Campaign buttons, stickers, and posters were used to advertise the messages of the candidates. Candidates gave stump speeches around the country, some traveling by car and others (e.g., Harry Truman) using a train to transport themselves from city to city.

For a long time, the president was considered to be the nation's preacher, cheerleader, and teacher. However, the age of television has enlarged this role. In the days of Truman or Lyndon Johnson, the government was really the tool used to address the country's problems. But the era of big government is over, and now problems have to be solved by the American people, with the president going over the head of Congress and appealing directly to each and every citizen.

Admittedly, the presidency today does not have the challenges it once did such as the Great Depression, World War II, and the cold war. Franklin D. Roosevelt pushed through the New Deal, Dwight Eisenhower halted the Korean conflict, and Johnson launched the Great Society. Ronald Reagan will be remembered for his role in cutting taxes, ending the cold war, and reforming the tax code. Words and symbols are especially important in this television era in which we live, for example, the constant smiles and demeanors of Reagan and Jimmy Carter selling well on television and lifting people's spirits. Reagan's "Morning in America," George Bush's "A Thousand Points of Light," and Bill Clinton's "Bridge to the 21st Century" are metaphors that seemed well designed for presidential image makers.[1]

Even presidential photographers complain of not being able to capture real-life moments anymore. Take, for example, the televised images of President Clinton's trip to Africa in the spring of 1998. Hundreds of thousands of people had surged forward, apparently with such force that the president had to yell at the top of his lungs to get people to move back. It was not a pretty sight, the president's face all red with anger as the sweat poured down his face in the raging heat. This was an unplanned photo opportunity that the White House did not want sent back home to the American people. To one photographer, Pete Souza of the *Chicago Tribune,* it was a pleasant sight. "For me, at least, it was somewhat refreshing to see the cameras catch Clinton in a candid, however uncomfortable, moment with the Ghana mob. You could almost feel the emotion as his temper erupted. It was a true human reaction."

Souza has recorded presidents in two roles, most recently one of many national press corps photographers and then as one of four official White House photographers during the Reagan era. He points out that what people see come out in print is not so much history in the making as it is a history lesson in manipulation. During Reagan's terms in office, Souza would need only a nod to one of Reagan's aides to get permission to walk into the Oval Office at any time to photograph whatever meeting the president was involved with at the time. According to Souza, no one told him which pictures he could or could not take so long as the routine ceremonial pictures were included. With this vantage point, Souza was able to see how Reagan's image handlers set the stage and presented him in just the right context for the rest of the world to observe him in action.

In the Clinton White House, where Souza occasionally has been invited to photograph the president, he sees the access as much more restrictive. Souza points out that rules dictate precisely which pictures can and cannot be taken. Souza adds that he thinks that Clinton is a much better actor than Reagan. "The Reagan I saw in private was much the same as the Reagan I saw in public. He was just playing himself on stage. With Clinton, though, it seems even his public emotions are an act."[2]

The packaging of politicians is not in any way limited to the United States, nor are their images always manufactured and delivered over television. Take the case of the dictator of Zaire, Mobutu Sese Seko, who was overthrown in 1997 by Laurent Desire-Kabila. The latter promised the people of his country a clean start and change from his predecessor's corrupt ways. It turns out that the change was more in the form of packaging than anything else. After getting into office, Desire-Kabila relied on the skills of Seko's former image maker, Diminique Sakombi Inongo, who was the person who almost single-handedly had turned Seko into a legend in his own country, in part by having him appear in a leopard skin cap everywhere he went. As the minister of information, Inongo created a cult following around the former leader of Zaire. For example, he had Seko's face printed on cloth and passed out to the poor to wear as clothing. It also was Inongo who had the whole nation referring to its leader as "the Father of the Nation" and "the Guide." Perhaps his most celebrated packaging campaign was when he changed the name of Zaire to Congo and forced people to change their European names to African names or risk going to prison. In a recent interview, the 57-year-old Inongo said, "I manage ideas. I conceive and propose them to the president."[3]

SIMPLY PUT, MARKETING IS . . .

Every dynamic organization knows that change is the engine of growth. The marketing challenge, then, lies in anticipating, adapting to, and generating fresh ideas that exploit change. Perhaps in no better words can one define exactly what marketing is.

Marketing is the process by which companies select customers, analyze their needs, and then develop product innovations, advertising, pricing, and distribution strategies on the basis of that information. In politics, the application of marketing centers on the same process, but the analysis of needs centers on voters and citizens; the product becomes a multifaceted combination of the politician himself or herself, the politician's image, and the platform the politician advocates, which is then promoted and delivered to the appropriate audience. Although price is not directly applicable to politics, there still is a value proposition the politician is offering to citizens and voters in return for their support, which can come in the form of votes, money, volunteer efforts, or even positive responses to a pollster about the politician.

Moving public opinion, the currency of the political marketplace, is now in the hands of technocrats, not politicians. Candidates no longer have to get the "nod" of the party elites to run for president. Today, it takes a good pollster, media strategist, and direct mail specialist, as well as a stable of consultants, to win the White House. Can any political office be bought? No, a candidate is not guaranteed to win, but any candidate with enough money and the right marketing strategy is guaranteed an audience to hear what he or she has to say and has a greatly increased chance of winning. Michael Huffington and Oliver North both proved that a political office cannot be bought, with each spending approximately $30 million on a failed bid for Congress in 1994 but in the process attracting a substantial following.

In the open primary race to replace outgoing California Governor Pete Wilson in 1998, two multimillionaires tried unsuccessfully to wrestle the Democratic nomination away from Lieutenant Governor Gray Davis, who himself spent close to $9 million on his campaign. Business tycoon Al Checchi and wealthy lawyer Jane Harman both failed in their bids, even after spending close to $30 million each. But then again, products also fail, even after multi-million-dollar advertising campaigns are waged.

Television advertising that enabled marketers to mass market the hula hoop and the pet rock are being used to mass market ideas to voters. The same telemarketing techniques used to sell the Vegematic food processor are being used to solicit millions of dollars from concerned citizens to support the political programs of various interest groups. Political parties have seen their power shift to the hands of consultants who represent the interest groups. It is the interest groups, through the use of this new technology, that have gained enormous power in the system.

A president, no different from a McDonald's or a Chrysler, must be able to anticipate needs and wants of the marketplace to be successful. However, in politics, the process is much more fluid, dynamic, and unpredictable because of the various forces and varied competitors. Attitudes of the consumers, or voters in this case, are constantly changing because people are exposed to the influence of the media constantly talking about the president and his policies. We do not see this taking place in the commercial marketplace, where only competitive ads in magazines, in newspapers, and on television replace the role of the news media as a source of information for people to find out about the product in question.

FROM CAMPAIGNING TO GOVERNING

It is one thing to convince voters during the course of a campaign that a candidate is an effective leader, and it is another thing to continue to be that convincing after entering the White House. A good campaigner must have his or her finger on the pulse of the people and be able to respond to public opinion. A good president, on the other hand, also must be able to understand the mood of the country and be able to move public opinion in the direction of the vision he or she creates, not just respond to it. A politician can be a great campaigner but a poor leader. Unfortunately, if the reverse is true, then the politician might not have the opportunity to prove himself or herself as a leader if the politician is not able to get elected.

Governing in Washington, D.C., has become more difficult because of the technological and structural changes that have taken place over the years. There is a gridlock in the nation's capital that has been permeated by the special interest groups and their influence peddling. Trying to bring campaign spending under control is now almost impossible because of the influence of the interest groups. Just look at the level of inaction on the part of Congress to pass campaign finance reform laws. The incumbents know that they could not win office without the help of fund-raisers that swell their coffers with money, both "soft" and "hard."[4]

THE MARKETING CHALLENGE
TO A SITTING PRESIDENT

Control of information becomes more difficult to a sitting president and not as easy to influence as it is during a campaign. Once in office, the president develops more enemies because the stakes are higher, and the impact of the president's decisions are greater in that they affect the entire free world. The competitive environment includes congressional leaders, talk radio hosts, world leaders, political action committees, interest groups, lobbies, and others that influence the job the president is doing. Because of the tendency of polls to bob up and down, and because of the torrent of information and persuasive messages coming out all the time about the president and his actions, it is incumbent on the president to maintain a vision so as not to be pushed from side to side of an issue, thereby projecting an image of a flip-flopper.

The polls and marketing research are tools used not only by the media to monitor the relative success of the president vis-à-vis his approval ratings but also by the president's inner circle of trusted advisers to determine the impact of every utterance out of the president's mouth. In addition, the polls are used to frame policy decisions to be sure that they will fly with the American people before they are put on the table. Presidential leadership has become reactionary, on the one hand, but also has forced presidents to more carefully consider the thoughts of the people in this country. Just witness the role that Dick Morris played in Clinton's final 2 years of his first term as president. Polling was constantly carried out to ensure that issues and policies that the president advocated were well received.[5] It is a paradox that needs to be discussed at length and in the open.

THE IMPACT OF TECHNOLOGY

Because of interactive communication technology and the capability of individuals who understand this new medium to affect the political agenda, the power of the political parties has been fractionalized into many smaller groups, each with influence on the thinking of the voters. Our democracy has become a decentralized, participatory form of government, where interest groups are able to vocalize and use their power by going direct to the public through the Internet on the information highway. The net result of this process is that the voters read about this in the daily polls that reflect the tug-and-pull and up-and-down nature of politics, leading to more disillusioned voters.

The information technology industry has spawned many cottage industries, with companies entering left and right. One example is a company called Bonner and Associates, which is able to send out 10,000 faxes overnight to a congressperson's office. When the firm is hired by a client, it isolates the "swing votes" in Congress, does a scan of the corresponding districts, and identifies citizens whose profiles suggest that they are sympathetic to the cause. Then, after a critical committee hearing in Congress, Bonner employees call the sympathetic citizens, explain what is happening, and (through the magic of telecommunications) put them directly in touch with the congressperson whose vote is critical to blockage or passage of the bill in question. The charge is $350 to $500 per call.[6]

In the future, we can expect technological advances to continue to have a profound effect on politics. Advances in the telecommunications industry, especially interactive technology, have the potential to transform the electoral process as we know it today into a more direct democracy. For example, it might become possible for citizens to vote from their own homes on their computers. On a positive note, this change brings with it the potential for substantially increasing the level of participation in presidential elections.

With the ever-present media coverage of politics today, from 24-hour CNN coverage to up-to-the-second coverage over the Internet, polls have become the most interesting aspect of politics on which journalists report. In fact, telecommunications technology, with its interactive capabilities, has made it even easier and more cost-effective to poll people all over the world. The poll puts a spin on news that turns politicians into winners and losers. It is easily consumed information by even the most uninterested citizen, and it is something that can be compared over and over again with new polls after they come out. This is a dangerous practice, but one that cannot be avoided with the "horse race" mentality that permeates our society.

MARKET-DRIVEN POLITICS

The 1992 presidential campaign was a watershed election in that it changed the rules of campaigning. Candidates relied on sophisticated technologies that allowed them to circumvent the traditional media and go direct to the voters. Clinton and Ross Perot relied on cable television, telecommunications advances, and satellite technology to target their messages and appeals to voters no differently from how toy manufacturers (e.g., Mattel) target their advertisements to children on Saturday morning cartoon shows. Just 4 years earlier, presidential candidates did not appear on MTV playing the saxophone, announce their candidacies on CNN's *Larry King Live* (as Perot did), use infomercials to get their messages out, or have debates in electronic town hall meeting settings.[7]

During each of Clinton's two presidential campaigns, he relied on focus groups and polls to direct his campaign strategy, which circumvented the traditional media and went directly to the voters. Perhaps more than any other single issue, it was Clinton's ability to follow a market orientation—which centers on a campaign built around voters' concerns and desires rather than his own—that enabled his message to get across as effectively as it did. A majority of the American electorate bought into Clinton's vision for America.[8]

Market-driven politics, along with all the campaign changes, brings with it a price that is revealed in polls that measure the degree to which Americans hold their president in high esteem. In a major study by the Center for Media and Public Affairs, it was determined that presidential candidates receive far more bad press than good press, leaving one with the impression that the media are in part to blame for the problem in the system. A generation ago, most Americans liked or admired the man they elected president. Lately, pollsters tell us that people regard their candidate as the lesser of two evils.

The challenge to the president lies with the fact that there are different interest groups, each with its own set of needs that a president has to attempt to satisfy. It is impossible to satisfy every interest group's needs, so careful marketing research is conducted to determine which issues are of more importance to each interest group. It is easy enough to use research to identify the needs of different groups of citizens during a campaign, but it is a very different challenge to get issues and policies passed through Congress after entering the White House. A president can be effective only if he is able to move legislation through Congress. As a president's approval ratings increase in the polls, there is indirect pressure on congresspersons and senators to work with the president to avoid alienating their constituencies.

Immediately after Clinton became president, a "permanent campaign" was launched in the White House. Just as the Clinton organization used the "war room" as the nerve center to monitor all of its strategic activities during the course of his two campaigns, so did the Clinton White House set up a war room to market its programs to the American people.

This raises a very serious issue about the way in which our democracy works. Just as we have attempted to educate consumers to be alert to the slick methods of some businesspeople (e.g., elderly people who fall prey to the persuasive tactics of fast-talking salespersons), so too must voters understand how our democracy works in this high-tech age. Candidates cannot win office without testing out different ideas during the primaries, just as presidents cannot win reelection without trying to compromise in responding to changing events.

However, just as companies have to be careful not to promise too much as they raise consumers' expectations, so too do politicians have to be careful not to raise the expectations of voters too high.

DEMOCRACY ON SHAKY GROUND

The White House and members of Congress have policies to push and elections to win. The press has a money-making motive and a public service obligation. These two goals have created a problem for democracy in this country. Although the interest of the two overlap, there tends to be a cynicism that is sapping people's confidence in politics and public officials and is eroding the standing and standards of journalism. Reporters cover government activity with the mind-set of horse race journalism that one would find in the heat of a campaign, always emphasizing who is winning or losing and not what is being done.

According to David Broder, a well-respected Washington correspondent, "With the political challenges and the decline of the parties, everything is so volatile [that] you need more control in the White House than perhaps you once did. The White House needs to be on top of everything that gets into the evening news level of attention." George Stephanapolous said,

> First of all, I agree that you do need control in the White House. . . . You cannot separate politics from government at all. There were some stories, even this week, about the endless campaign. There is no way around it. Right now, we have 24-hour news cycles. . . . CNN [ensures] that you are forced to react at any time, and that's going to happen throughout the time of the Clinton presidency. The toughest part of this is discipline. And I think that is going to be the hardest thing we have to grapple with. We have to have discipline to decide what we want to do, to build a consensus to do it, and then to stick by it once it's done.[9]

The fact remains that the power of the political party in the United States has been diminished. What has influenced this is the absence of patronage armies and strong partisan leadership as well as the advent of sophisticated, costly media strategies in campaigns, which have lowered the value of the political party endorsement. In some cases, being a part of a slate assembled by party leaders could be a liability for candidates. But this is not to minimize the continual reservoir of money that political parties have to distribute to candidates running for all levels of office.

Kevin Philips, a noted political analyst, believes that the two-party system no longer works because Washington is dominated by an entrenched bureaucracy, with influential power brokers holding the purse strings to put politicians in office. Philips is convinced that the problem is systemic, with Rome, Constantinople, and Madrid as examples of other powers that fell because of abuses of power. The solution, he says, is to have Congress operate from other parts of the country in addition to Washington, establish a system to have national referenda, and take aim at the abusive forces in Washington. Philips questions who will set such reforms in motion along with the dropping of political attack advertisements. He points to the congresspersons who regularly leave office, sometimes willingly, to become Washington lobbyists.[10]

The great disgust with the two-party system has opened the door to the possibility of a third-party candidate having a real shot at the presidency. This happened in 1992 when Colin Powell, a popular Gulf War hero, was shown to be a front-runner before he decided not to run. Of course, one has to keep in mind that the last time a third-party candidate won was when the new Republican Party supplanted the Whigs and the Republican candidate, Abraham Lincoln, captured the White House in 1860. Since then, only once has a third-party candidate even finished second, and that was in 1912, when ex-President Theodore Roosevelt did it campaigning as a Progressive and received 28% of the vote.[11]

The fact remains that today, any message initiated by anyone can be picked up and carried on the Internet, on television, or on talk radio, bringing with it a whole new life and meaning other than what was intended and, at the same time, greatly distorting an issue.[12]

The United States prides itself on being a model of participatory democracy. But according to a new study, America lags behind much of the world when it comes to casting ballots. An average of just 44.1% of the voting-age population has turned out for national legislative elections during the 1990s, putting the United States in 139th place among 163 countries surveyed by the International Institute for Democracy and Electoral Assistance. The voting percentages of some other countries are as follows: Sweden 83.2%, Denmark 81.1%, Israel 78.4%, Spain 77.6%, Britain 75.4%, Germany 72.7%, Finland 68.5%, Canada 63.9%, France 61.3%, and Japan 56.6%. If one measure of the strength of a democracy is determined by the proportion of people who participate in the choice of their leaders, then changes definitely need to be made in the United States.[13]

THE INCREASING POWER OF POLITICAL ACTION COMMITTEES

The 1996 presidential campaign was witness to the influence that interest groups carry in politics today. For example, the fact that the social conservatives were able to direct the development of the campaign platform in the Republican Party reveals a gradual shift that has been taking place over the past several years, moving the power from brokers in the party to brokers in critical interest groups such as the Christian Coalition. From a marketing perspective, the movement of power into the hands of interest groups puts even more pressure on politicians to rely on pollsters in an effort to better understand the needs and wants of these influential constituencies because they are in a position to influence both the communication and delivery of a politician's message.

According to Gary Bauer, president of the Family Research Council, the growth of the Republican Party is among people who are concerned with what has happened to American values. In 1996, candidates who supported abortion rights, such as California Governor Wilson and Pennsylvania Senator Arlen Specter, were early casualties of the primary process.[14]

To get a feel for the raw power of one interest group, the Christian Coalition, one simply needs to look at how the group members promoted their ideas. Ralph Reed, the former director of the Christian Coalition, indicated that the group registered 1 million new voters before the November election and distributed approximately 17 million congressional scorecards rating members of Congress on how they voted on issues important to conservatives. The coalition also distributed some 45 million voter guides comparing candidates' stands. As a tax-exempt, nonprofit lobbying organization, the coalition can publish information about issues but not endorse individual candidates. The problem here is that there is not any reporting of the sources of the money of the coalition because, technically, it is not a political action committee.[15]

Another influential interest group is the American Association of Retired Persons (AARP). In one of its programs, the AARP carried out a community outreach program in which volunteers in 41 states conducted 2-hour seminars at their local senior centers, libraries, and hospitals. The outreach programs were open to the public and provided voters with information about the AARP's key election year issues. In addition, volunteers distributed voter guides, sponsored candidate forums, and help to register voters for the general election.[16]

In the 1996 presidential campaign, the sheer power of association with the Christian Coalition pushed Bob Dole to send his vice presidential nominee, Jack Kemp, to attend its annual "Road to Victory" celebration. The move was meant to distance Dole from the religious right in his desire to broaden his appeal to a wider spectrum of voters. The fact of the matter is that the evangelical Protestants make up the core of the Christian Coalition and other religious right organizations, which amounts to approximately 24% of the voting electorate, up from 19% in 1987, according to a recent study by the Pew Research Center. The Pew study reported that 42% of the White evangelicals identify themselves as Republican. At a local level, the Christian Coalition carefully placed its members onto school boards and city councils. The coalition's breakthrough in national elections came in 1994, when members distributed millions of pro-Republican voter guides that helped the Republican Party gain control of Congress after 40 years in the minority. Its reward was a regular meeting with top Republican politicians. According to the U.S. Postal Service, the organization mailed 310,296 copies of its *Christian American* magazine, which goes to people who contribute at least $15 a month to the group. Tax returns of donations to the coalition totaled $18.7 million in 1995, off nearly 12% from the $21.2 million it collected in 1994.[17]

A year before the 1996 election, the Clinton-Gore campaign began running ads on Christian radio stations in 15 states touting the president's support for the anti-gay marriage legislation passed by Congress in August. Interestingly, after receiving complaints from gay groups, Clinton pulled the ads off the air.[18] One person who has run a single-handed campaign against the Christian right is Walter Cronkite, who sent our letters to 450,000 homes around the country calling for support against the growing influence of the religious right. In one part of the letter, Cronkite wrote about the Christian right as having "a militant ideology—one that encourages deep hostility toward those who disagree with its agenda." One organization that has sought to counter the rising influence of the Christian right is the Interfaith Alliance, which has promoted itself as a middle-of-the-road alternative to the Christian Coalition. Cronkite's letter on behalf of the Interfaith Alliance immediately brought in about $100,000 and 7,000 new members. Ideas for this group were conceived in 1994 by a Jewish political consultant and a Catholic political researcher. As of 1997, the alliance had about 40,000 supporters, nowhere near the 1.7 million supporters the Christian Coalition had in more than 100 chapters in 36 states. Most of the issues of the Alliance have been local ones. The alliance is made up of Presbyterians, Baptists, Methodists, Episcopalians, Catholics, Muslims, and Jewish people.[19]

SOCIETAL PRESSURES AND THE NEED FOR MARKETING

In a study of voters by the Wirthlin Group in 1995, 60% of the respondents revealed that they feel the problems facing the country are "primarily moral and social in nature" as opposed to "primarily economic in nature." Three out of four Americans believe that the country is in a state of moral decay, and 84% want government policies to be directed by moral values. If we go back to the period from 1960 to 1990, the rate of illegitimacy rose by 94%, the rate of divorce rose by 125%, and the rate of violent crime rose by 358%. In a study of the religious conduct of Americans, it was found that only 26% of Americans defined their religious orientation as conservative, 44% defined it as moderate, and the rest either defined it as liberal or refused to be categorized.[20]

Along with the increased concern with morals in this country is a decrease of 40% to 50% in the number of people who are devoting time to community affairs such as attending rallies and working for political parties. For example, during the 1950s, 75% of Americans indicated that they trusted the government in Washington to do what is right most of the time. However, that same attitude now stands at barely 20%. Community ties among people also have become weaker. Men's groups (e.g., Elks, Moose, Eagles) and women's organizations (e.g., League of Women Voters, Federations of Women Clubs) have seen membership fall by 25% to 60% over the past two decades.[21]

Of course, the real question is whether there is an incentive to change the current political system. During the 1996 presidential campaign, the nation's top 75 media markets took in $400 million in political advertising, which was up from $300 million in 1992, according to Competitive Media Reporting, an ad industry research firm. A total of $4 billion was spent on all elections in 1996.

In her book, *Facing Up to the American Dream: Race, Class, and the Soul of the Nation,* Jennifer L. Hochschild makes the point that the "American Dream" has long been pursued by Americans but currently is not easily attainable by many. Hochschild defines the dream as "the promise that all Americans have a reasonable chance to achieve success as they define it, material or otherwise, through their own efforts and to attain virtue and fulfillment through success."[22]

According to a poll conducted by Yankilovich Partners for *The New Yorker* among 1,200 African American adults, three out of five Black Americans feel that their conditions are worsening, and a like proportion think that the American Dream has become impossible to achieve. Interestingly, these beliefs cut across social classes. Fully 58% say that their conditions are getting worse, whereas 59% agree that the American Dream has become impossible for most to achieve.[23] The American Dream used to be a decent job, a chance to use one's talents, membership in a community, a reasonably secure future, a house, a car, and some money in the bank to see the kids through school and to provide for retirement.[24]

As the gap between the "haves" and "have-nots" in the United States continues to widen to a point where it is greater than in other Western countries, the political pressures to respond to this reality increase. It also puts the have-nots at a disadvantage at representing themselves through interest groups because they simply do not have the money to sustain the effective promotional campaign necessary to get their points across. Federal Reserve figures indicate that in 1989, the richest 1% of U.S. households owned nearly 40% of the nation's wealth. Their net worth started at $2.3 million. In Britain, by comparison, the richest 1% possessed 18% of that nation's wealth. The top 20% of U.S. households, families with a net worth of $180,000 or more, had 80% of the wealth, a bigger share than in any other industrial nation. In Finland, where distribution of income is particularly even, the lowest-earning 20% of the population gets 10.8% of the income. In the United States, the figure is only 5.7%. Inequality has risen in the United States since the 1970s. There are many explanations for this inequality including rising automation, the elimination of unskilled jobs, and a low minimum wage.[25]

WASHINGTON GOES HOLLYWOOD

Hollywood has been eager to capture the fascination with the power and intrigue associated with the White House. Clinton ultimately might be remembered as the president who was in the White House when film after film was made about him. In some cases, the fantasy created in the movies came very close to the reality after the fact. The president has been turned into an action hero, as he was depicted in *Air Force One* by Harrison Ford and in *Independence Day* by Bill Pullman. Although it is not new for Hollywood to expose the corruption that exists in American politics, it is now being played out in a far more brutal and sensational way than it was in the past. For example, in the 1942 film *Yankee Doodle Dandy,* George M. Cohan, played by James Cagney, meets President Franklin D. Roosevelt, a man depicted as wise and mature. In the 1960s film, *Sunrise at Campobello,* Roosevelt is depicted again, this time by Ralph Bellamy, as a decent and fair president. Who would have ever thought of making a movie about Roosevelt and his mistress, Lucy Mercer Rutherford, or about Eisenhower and his mistress, Kay Summersby, or about John F. Kennedy and all of his mistresses. These indiscretions were not even mentioned by the press. The same cannot be said for Clinton.[26]

First, we were given the movie *Dave,* in which Kevin Kline impersonates the president as a friendly look-alike when the real president suffers a stroke while fooling around with a woman in a hotel. Only 2 years later, *The American President,* played by Michael Douglas, is a story about a widower who has a rocky courtship with a lobbyist. Next came the movie *Wag the Dog,* in which a president manufacturers a war to shift the media attention away from one of his romantic liaisons. In *Primary Colors,* John Travolta, in an uncannily close resemblance to Clinton, plays President Jack Stanton, a southern President who is willing to do anything it takes to win over the hearts and minds of the American people. Hollywood has capitalized on not only a fascination but a voyeurism that the American people seem to have with inner workings of the White House.[26]

Washington has become the Hollywood of the East, where image is more important than substance and the intensity of a politician's charisma determines his power with the people. The rise of celebrity culture puts new demands on a celebrity presidency. The president of today has become America's celebrity-in-chief.

There currently is a communications revolution taking place that puts the president into the living rooms of ordinary citizens on a daily basis. If one were to go back to the presidency of Franklin D. Roosevelt, it was not a known fact that he was confined to a wheelchair because of his affliction with polio. Nor did people know about the relationship with his mistress. Kennedy was the first real celebrity president who was watched by the American people on television every day. Since that time, the office of the presidency never has been the same. Presidents now communicate visually with the American people, manipulating their appearance, words, and actions to communicate a particular message and to create an image in a consistent manner.

The one president since the television era who mastered the correct balance of exposure was Reagan, who was under constant control by his handlers. Michael Deaver, Reagan's image maker, was careful to use the media in a very controlled manner, skillfully manipulating the symbols of the office such as the Rose Garden, Air Force One, and even the American flag that became a centerpiece for each of his campaigns. Reagan used television to stress the majesty of the office, unlike Carter, who after Watergate tried to downplay the office. But the one president who has mastered the use of marketing in this age of manufactured images is Clinton.[27]

MONEY AND POLITICS

The desire to have influence in a democratic society is part of the human nature of every political player. However, it is the duty of the politicians in power to ensure that the level of that influence is restrained by the laws and doctrines of a society. The fact of the matter is that in an open society, where there is no limit on how much an individual can spend on a campaign out of his or her own pocket, the level of spending can have a dramatic impact on the outcome of an election. Because marketing efforts are centered around the development and delivery of images and information, money can play a critical role in the process.

During the 1996 campaign cycle in the United States, at least $660 million was spent by candidates and parties looking to win seats in both the Senate and House of Representatives. The average Senate campaign now costs approximately $4.5 million, with each senator having to raise at least $14,000 every week of his or her 6-year term to pay for the expenses of running for reelection. The only other democracy where as much money is spent on campaigns is Japan, where candidates, and not political parties, are in a position of having to fund their own elections.[28]

Unfortunately, in the United States, we always are "behind the 8-ball" trying to revamp the election laws to keep up with the changing technology and communications infrastructure that influences campaigns so greatly. Several countries have seen governments fall due to campaign spending infractions, for example, the Liberal Democrats in Japan in 1993 and the Italian political elite in 1992.[28]

The natural question to ask is why so much money is needed to run campaigns. Many would say that the answer lies in the television era in which we live and the need to pay for the exorbitant costs of running commercials. In Britain, the political parties are not allowed to buy commercials on television. As a result, most political advertising is done on billboards. However, in the United States, as a result of the fact that there is a desire on the part of the electorate to get its political information over television, that is where the candidates put their messages. In many European countries, the political parties finance most of the cost of a campaign, which ultimately comes from money subsidized by the taxpayers.

In the United States, candidates are in a position where they have to raise funds for their campaigns on their own. Only 12% of taxpayers in 1998 checked off the box indicating that they were willing to contribute a few dollars to the political parties, which is one indication of the low esteem with which politics is held in the citizens' minds. The rising cost of elections also is resulting from the price tags of highly paid political consultants, who have absorbed some of the influence that the party bosses used to wield. Due to the 24-hour news coverage we have of every move and sound bite issued by a candidate, there must be a team ready to fire back at any accusations that are made. And due to the fact that there are no laws prohibiting what a politician can say in a political commercial, the rapid-fire back and forth is virtually out of control in the United States today. Candidates have to spend money just to keep their own names and records cleansed from the slander that is thrown at them by political opponents.[28]

Incumbents in the United States enjoy a great advantage when it comes to raising money. In 1996, incumbents received four times as much money as their challengers, and in nearly every case, those who spent more money won. This also was true in 1994, when more than 90% of the incumbents who sought reelection won. Once a candidate wins, the money tree begins to grow bigger and bigger as political favors begin to be paid back with support in the form of money. So, the real question is whether democracy is strengthened or weakened by all this spending. Ultimately, there are two basic approaches (which I elaborate on later in the book) that can be taken to deal with the problem: limiting the supply of money in the form of donations or limiting the need for money in the form of spending. In many democracies around the world, the playing field is leveled out by giving public finances in proportion to the number of seats a party holds. This is true in Japan, Germany, France, Spain, and Belgium. But as we know from scandals that have hit Japan, this alone will not always work, especially if an individual is allowed to spend one's own money on a campaign.[28]

Some European nations limit donations to those from individuals and ban them from organizations or corporations. For example, in Belgium, donations from either companies or unions are banned, and in Germany, donations from unions are banned. Still, loopholes always can be found in nearly every system. Many in the United States are in favor of banning soft money, where it is more difficult to trace the origins of contributions. Even when it is possible to trace the sources of funds that have been illegally contributed, the Federal Election Commission is so strapped for funds itself (similar to the Federal Trade Commission that oversees corporate spending on advertising and regulates on deceptive practices by corporations) that it takes many years to identify and punish the wrongdoing that occurs. At the heart of the problem is a Supreme Court ruling in 1976, *Buckley v. Valeo,* that equates free speech with the money it takes to get a message out to the American people as well as the First Amendment right to free speech in this country.[28]

At the core of this discussion is the issue of disclosure, both on the part of those who contribute and on the part of those who put the commercials on the air. Connected to this issue is the importance of holding someone or an organization accountable as well for what is said in political commercials. Currently, candidates are required to reveal how much money they raise, where they received the money, and how much of it was spent. People who give money to politicians or candidates seeking office have to make their names public. Even those who spend money independently to promote candidates must file reports with the Federal Election Commission. The Supreme Court upheld these regulations in 1976, when it decided that disclosure would both help the electorate to make judgments about a candidate and, at the same time, deter corruption. The trade-off in many people's minds is putting greater demands on disclosure instead of limiting spending.[29]

CONCLUSION

Our electoral system originally was set up to give candidates the opportunity to let voters know who they are and what they stand for during the course of a primary campaign. However, an interesting twist has taken place in politics today. Through the use of scientific polling, candidates now use marketing research to do just the opposite, that is, to find out who the voters are and what they want the candidates to stand for. Candidates can then feed back to the voters the ideas that they know will sell in the marketplace. With the recent advances in digital communications, voters in this country are so well wired in to the federal government that interest groups have the power to change legislation in a matter of days. With lobbyists sitting in the balconies of Congress listening to debates on issues sensitive to their interest groups, all it takes is one call on a lobbyist's cellular phone to initiate a letter-writing campaign to flood a congressperson's office with enough mail to stop the politician dead in his or her tracks. This is direct democracy, but is it good? The answer is a flat *no* if we look at how the Constitution set up our government. According to our Founding Fathers, the idea was to have a body of lawmakers who were indifferent to the ebb and flow of public opinion and who could sit back and deliberate in their chambers about the wisdom of issues and policies. This no longer is possible with the impact that marketing has had on democracy.

Television programs such as *Nightline, This Week With David Brinkley, Meet the Press, Larry King Live,* and *Crossfire* help to set the public agenda and, in some cases, even serve as platforms for presidential candidacies, as we saw in the case of Perot in 1992. Candidates in 1992 transformed entertainment events into political events by appearing on programs such as *Larry King Live* and Arsenio Hall's talk show. This created a confusion between entertainment and politics, partly the result of news being driven today by entertainment value.

The problem with this type of government is that the public does not get the basic information it needs, the government does not get the support it deserves, and the press finds itself drawn into a downward spiral of cheapened values and lost respect. So, what should the role of the media be? Radio talk shows, television programs, and supermarket tabloids have huge audiences and have been successful at winning over large numbers of people. A Times/Mirror poll indicated that 21% of the American public believe that politicians set the agenda, whereas 43% think that the media set the agenda. This is reflected in the fact that there is great competition among the press, television, radio, and other reporters to outdo one another to provide the news. It is simply that politics and polls make for better news than do policies. According to David Shaw, the *Los Angeles Times* media reporter, "The media have not only blurred the lines between responsible journalism and sensationalism, they have undermined their own integrity and credibility, and worse, they have given readers and viewers an increasingly distorted picture of their society and of themselves."[30]

In 1994, campaign finance specialist Stan Huckaby's firm, Huckaby and Associates, conducted a study of previous spending on presidential campaigns in both parties since 1976. According to the results, the candidate who raised the most money in the year preceding the general election (with the exception of one Republican primary candidate in 1980) went on to win the nomination. Since the campaign reforms of 1974, which limited contributions to $1,000 for individuals and $5,000 for political committees and which preempted wealthy individuals from bankrolling presidential campaigns, presidential candidates have been thrown into the laps of political consultants and direct mail specialists. In other words, without a sizable war chest to direct the marketing activities, it has become almost impossible to become president in the United States.

In politics, there is an information overload, with a negative slant on the product by the media. This has perpetuated the negative attitudes on the part of the voters, making the job of manufacturing constructive, positive images that much more difficult for politicians to sell and even more difficult to get the American public to buy.

The proportion of Americans who trust their leaders has plummeted from the 70% level of the 1960s to approximately 20% during the mid-1990s.[31] Is this a reaction to the alienation fostered by the turn toward negative campaigning and mean-spirited attacks on our politicians? Is it the reaction to politicians who refuse to stand up and go "against" the polls if they feel strongly about an issue? Or, is it in response to a political system that has lost control of what it is doing and reflective of a loss of power of the political party? The answer to all of these questions is *yes.*

Welcome to politics in the age of manufactured images, where the polls and pundits control the voters and the candidates and where politics has taken on an air of commercialism that is dangerously close to becoming too reactionary and too "in touch." The real American national game is politics, not baseball. From early childhood onward, every citizen is taught the rules, learns the names of the past and present superstars, and is urged to take part. But today, it is a game increasingly played, coached, and managed from the local sandlot elections up through the major leagues by professional marketers. They bring to the field an assortment of the specialized communication skills, market-proven selling tactics, and media-handling abilities that are the necessary components of a successful campaign. For all practical purposes, marketing is now the name of the game, and political consultants are the coaches and managers who determine the outcome, with the media serving as umpires.

NOTES

1. Neikirk, W. (1997a, January 20). Bully pulpit renews its power. *Chicago Tribune,* sec. 1, pp. 1, 13.

2. Souza, P. (1998, April 5). Decisive moments are few when you must capture history on cue. *Chicago Tribune* (Perspective), pp. 1, 10.

3. Block, R. (1998, February 9). Congo's name is new, but one face looks a bit familiar. *Wall Street Journal,* pp. A1, A10.

4. The distinction between soft and hard money stems from the regulations on contributions that the Federal Election Commission (FEC) imposes on candidates running for political office. Hard money contributions are subject to restrictions delineated in the FEC amendments of 1971 and 1974. Soft money contributions are marginally unregulated with respect to the limits that are imposed on candidates. For example, a candidate running for the presidency may have a political action committee at the state

level that brings in contributions subject to FEC regulations. In that sense, these are hard money contributions because there are limits on how much money an organization or individual can contribute to a candidate's campaign. However, the hard money contribution turns into a soft money contribution when the candidate's state organization passes that money on to the national campaign organization.

5. Morris, D. (1997). *Behind the Oval Office: Winning the presidency in the nineties*. New York: Random House.

6. Wright, R. (1995, January 23). Hyper democracy. *Time*, p. 18.

7. Newman, B. I. (1994). *The marketing of the president: Political marketing as campaign strategy*. Thousand Oaks, CA: Sage.

8. Newman, B. I. (1993, June). The role of marketing in the 1992 U.S. presidential election: How Bill Clinton was transformed from "Slick Willie" to "Mr. President." *Werbeforschung & Praxis*, pp. 195-201.

9. Broder, D. (1994, April 6). From the campaign trail, timely words for the White House. *Chicago Tribune*, sec. 1, p. 15.

10. Begley, A. (1995, October 8). Serious play [book review]. *Chicago Tribune*, sec. 14, pp. 1-2.

11. Ullmann, O. (1995, May 22). Maybe even the general can't outflank the two-party system. *Business Week*, pp. 57-58.

12. Warren, J. (1995, May 14). No more shades of gray. *Chicago Tribune*, sec. 5, p. 2.

13. Malanowski, J. (1997, August 4). The celluloid senator. *Time*, p. 18.

14. Tackett, M. (1996, August 9). Right-wing rules on GOP platform. *Chicago Tribune*, sec. 1, pp. 1, 24.

15. Jacoby, M. (1996a, September 14). Christian Coalition rally bashes Democrats. *Chicago Tribune*, sec. 1, p. 3.

16. *AARP Voter*. (1996, Fall). [whole issue].

17. Jacoby, M. (1996b, September 13). Signs hint Christian Coalition influence has peaked. *Chicago Tribune*, sec. 1, pp. 1, 24.

18. Krauthammer, C. (1996, October 28). And that's the truth—Sort of. *Chicago Tribune*, sec. 1, p. 15.

19. Haynes, D. (1997, March 9). Alliance responds to Christian right. *Chicago Tribune*, sec. 1, p. 4.

20. Etzioni, A. (1995, September 13). The politics of morality. *Wall Street Journal*, p. A14.

21. Putnam, R. D. (1996, January 10). Why we're on our worst behavior. *Chicago Tribune*, sec. 1, p. 17.

22. Drew, B. (1995, October 15). Dream interpretation [book review]. *Chicago Tribune*, sec. 14, p. 5.

23. Associated Press. (1996b, April 22). Most Blacks say American Dream impossible to achieve, poll finds. *Chicago Tribune*, sec. 1, p. 1.

24. Longworth, R. C. (1966, April 28). The dream, in pieces: America's economic woes are becoming a crisis of spirit. *Chicago Tribune*, sec. 2, pp. 15-20.

25. Associated Press. (1995a, April 18). Gap between rich, poor greatest in U.S., studies find. *Chicago Tribune,* sec. 1, p. 13.

26. Lacayo, R. (1998, March 16). All the president's movies: Musclehead or sex fiend—The image of the chief executive is no longer a winning ticket. *Time,* pp. 72-73.

27. Neikirk, W. (1997b, January 26). Celebrity in chief: Reverence or fodder for the soaps? *Chicago Tribune,* sec. 2, pp. 1, 13.

28. Money and politics: Politicians for rent. (1997, February 8). *The Economist,* pp. 23-25.

29. Chapman, S. (1995, May 7). Sneak attack. *Chicago Tribune,* sec. 4, p. 3.

30. Broder, D. (1994, February 23). Who will sort out true from false if the media can't? *Chicago Tribune,* sec. 1, p. 19.

31. See Wright (Note 6).

2

From Party Politics to Mass Marketing

Politics is the art of acquiring, holding, and wielding power.
—Indira Gandhi, 1975

If we look at presidential elections before 1952, politics operated on the principle of machine politics. Party bosses in smoke-filled back rooms would choose the candidates and decide the platforms. Candidates then relied on the national party organization and help from local and state party officials to coordinate their campaigns. One-to-one contact with the voters usually was orchestrated by the political party in each community and consisted of glad-handing events.

The emergence of television was the first opportunity for candidates to develop campaign platforms that revolved around the crafting of political images. Visual aids allowed candidates to craft careful images of themselves that would sell their ideas to the electorate. And instead of individual meetings with a couple hundred supporters, candidates could talk to thousands of constituents at a time. The power and reach of the new medium was amazing.

The introduction of television turned politics into the real national pastime. Furthermore, since the introduction of a longer primary season in 1972, the conventions have lost most of their suspense, turning them into tightly controlled "infomercials" lasting several days. They are run like Hollywood productions, with each participant exposed to the media following a tightly written script, called "talking points." Others have referred to the conventions as a miniseries for the political parties, whose aim is to paint a picture of the presidential and vice presidential nominees in as positive a light as possible. It is interesting to note that in 1960, 8 out of 10 households watched the conventions; in 1992, fewer than 4 out of 10 tuned in. In effect, the conventions became the major opportunity for the political parties to transform an otherwise unknown candidate into a household name, similar to what Procter & Gamble does through its commercials to introduce consumers to, say, a new bar of soap.[1]

In 1952, Dwight Eisenhower became the first presidential candidate to use television. In support of his bid for the presidency, he broadcast a series of commercials titled "Eisenhower Answers America." They featured a stiff and stone-faced Eisenhower haltingly reading cue cards in answer to questions from actors posing as typical voters. The result appears humorous by today's standards in its awkwardness and naïveté and is a far cry from the slick and sophisticated commercials we see today in political campaigns. Yet, at that time, it was effective.

Here is a sample:

Woman: You know what things cost today. High prices are just driving me crazy.

Eisenhower: Yes. My Mamie gets after me about the high cost of living. It's another reason why I say, it's time for a change. [Sound familiar?]

Man: I'm a veteran, General. What's wrong down in Washington? Graft, scandal, headlines. How can you fix it? [Again, sound familiar?]

Eisenhower: Here's how. By your votes, we'll get rid of the people who are too small for their jobs, too big for their britches.

The watershed year for modern-day political marketing was 1960. The televised debates that took place that year between John F. Kennedy and Richard Nixon ushered in a reliance on Madison Avenue advertising experts who coached both candidates in the fine art of media manipulation. In fact, many argued that were it not for television, Kennedy—the more telegenic and relaxed-looking candidate—would not have won. People who listened to the infamous debate on radio thought that Nixon won, and those who saw it on television believed that Kennedy won. For Nixon, the combination of shifting eyes and pearls of sweat on his upper lip killed his image. In his book, *The Making of the President,* Theodore White introduced the American people to the importance of centering energies in a campaign around the development of a superior product, in this case, Kennedy.[2]

Lyndon Johnson's 1964 presidential campaign against Barry Goldwater furthered the impact of television advertising and became the initial attempt at negative advertising. Goldwater, at the time, was perceived by the American electorate as "trigger happy" when it came to the use of nuclear weapons. Johnson's campaign was fueled by a controversial commercial depicting a little girl picking the petals off a daisy that suddenly turned into a nuclear bomb. Known as the "Daisy" commercial, it was considered so offensive that it ran only once during the campaign. However, Goldwater felt the impact. He came into the campaign with the image of a war monger who would be a trigger-happy president. In the spot, a young girl plucks daisy petals, counting and (in a nice touch of verisimilitude) miscounting as she goes. She is actually kind of cute and appealing looking, with her youth, innocence, and charm connoting nice things including peace, life, and a happy future. Then the camera zooms in for a tight close-up on the girl's face. Her voice dissolves into that of a man counting down for a missile launch, and her eye dissolves into the image of a mushroom cloud. Johnson's voice, folksy and reassuring, comes in: "These are the stakes: to make a world in which all of God's children can live or to go into the dark. We must either love each other or we must die."

The Johnson commercial represented a change in the nature of political advertising. Whereas on the surface, it was a powerful antiwar message, at a more subtle level, it reminded people of what they knew about Goldwater, who had characterized the atomic bomb as "merely another weapon." Johnson was one of the first to understand the value and effectiveness of symbolism to engage people's emotions, an important factor in voter decision making. Some have said it was the beginning of modern-day political advertising.

The presidential bid of Nixon in 1968 introduced the political world to the growing influence of Madison Avenue. Learning from his mistakes in the 1960 campaign and relying on advertising experts from the business world, Nixon incorporated the latest technological developments used to market products in his effort to communicate the image of an experienced politician. Nixon polished his political image through sophisticated political commercials, and then, starting a trend that would continue with successive presidencies, he invited his Madison Avenue handlers, John Haldeman and John Erlichman, into the inner sanctums of the White House to serve in high-level advisory positions. Joe McGinniss reported on this development quite succinctly in his book, *The Selling of the President*.[3]

The 1968 campaign turned into a bitter media fight between Nixon and Hubert Humphrey. Nixon cleverly used the media to soften his image, which one could characterize as lacking warmth and humor. Through trial and error during the course of the campaign, Nixon and his people quickly learned the importance of television and the media as campaign tools. The Nixon camp employed pollsters and ghostwriters to develop its successful advertising campaign. This was the first election in which the candidates were advertised and sold like products to the American people. The end result was the blending of

Nixon, the person and the legend, into someone who loomed larger than life and was much more interesting than the person himself. American politicians had turned the corner from simply presenting themselves to the electorate to presenting themselves as media personalities.[4]

THE BICENTENNIAL YEAR
AND BIG CHANGES

The campaign reforms of the early 1970s led to changes in campaign strategy. The Federal Election Campaign Act of 1971 (FECA) limited campaign expenditures and required disclosure of campaign expenditures. Along with several new stipulations, it called for the itemization of expenses exceeding $200 or more and the listing of contributors giving at least $200.[5] In addition, the reforms led to a longer prenomination campaign period, which increased costs to campaign organizations and pressured them to hire outside consultants. The new expanded primary season put pressure on candidates to use the latest marketing research technology to position and target appeals of concern in each primary state.

The 1976 campaign was the first presidential campaign regulated by the reforms, which fueled Jimmy Carter's victory over Gerald Ford. Working within the new guidelines and, at the same time, taking advantage of new reforms instituted in 1971, Pat Caddell, Carter's pollster, used a sophisticated marketing approach to campaigning and masterminded Carter's election victory. Using a technique called "market segmentation," in which the marketer identifies the needs of different audiences, isolates the unique benefits of his or her product, and then targets specific segments with different advertising appeals, Caddell helped Carter to win a much longer primary season by sending the appropriate message in each state where the candidate campaigned. For example, in Illinois, Carter appealed to the poor by advocating welfare reform and appealed to African Americans by promoting the idea of equal opportunity for all citizens.

It also was a year that earmarked a change in political advertising. Leading up to the 1976 election, there was some growth in the use of carefully crafted commercials in which the candidates themselves did not speak or make appearances. But ironically, in the 1976 campaign, there was a return by both Carter and Ford to old-fashioned personal appeals and the emergence of personal testimonies.

Ford's "I'm Feeling Good About America" commercial in 1976 associated the candidate with Norman Rockwellian images of Americans laughing, living, and raising the flag. "There's a change that's come over and is great to see" go the lyrics of the catchy tune that accompanies the Ford spot. "We're livin' here in peace again. We're goin' back to work again. It's better than it used to be."

"THE GREAT COMMUNICATOR" AND
BRINGING IT ALL TOGETHER

The 1980s introduced the American electorate to the age of electronic electioneering. This new form of political marketing used advances in the telecommunications industry and relied heavily on television to move campaigning into a new hi-tech mode. Candidates were pushed further into the laps of specialists who understood how to harness the power of telemarketing techniques.

In 1980, presidential candidate Ronald Reagan introduced the American electorate to a more sophisticated use of marketing. A former actor, Reagan had decades of experience working in front of the camera and knew how to use the medium to his advantage. Reagan's many years of acting proved to be a real asset in this new age of electronic electioneering, especially in the 1984 campaign against Walter Mondale, who looked stiff and ill at ease in front of the camera. Reagan's campaign organization represented a well-oiled marketing machine that relied on simple themes, such as patriotism and family, to convey one, single, consistent image at every campaign stop and in every commercial.

The Reagan presidency marked the real beginning of the integration of several marketing tools developed over a 40-year period including negative advertising, direct mail, sophisticated marketing research and polling, and planning and implementation of campaign strategy that closely mirrored what business was doing in the commercial marketplace.

Reagan's pollster, Richard Wirthlin, understood the significance of running a presidential campaign on the basis of information generated from focus groups and nationwide polls. In fact, it was here that we saw a meaningful leap from the use of polling to that of marketing research. Marketing research differs from polling by going beyond simple predictions of who someone would vote for to explaining the reasoning behind the person's choice. Armed with new information, Wirthlin helped Reagan and his consultant, Michael Deaver, to promote an image of Reagan as a strong leader who genuinely cared about the country.

Bringing together information technology with promotional expertise enabled both the 1980 and 1984 Reagan campaign organizations to craft specific images to targeted audiences. Part of the marketing evolution during this era used a powerful technique known as negative advertising. Introduced in 1964 by Johnson and his "Daisy" ad, this type of advertising is characterized by attacking the opponent rather than just promoting the candidate. Roger Ailes, Reagan's media adviser, put together commercials that effectively destroyed the opponent and, at the same time, built up Reagan.

Reagan's reelection campaign was a study in the power of rhetoric and incumbency as a way of preempting the Democratic challenges in an area where the Republicans might have been vulnerable. This election also represented the old politics versus the new politics. Reagan operated on the marketing concept, using technology, consumer research, and brand reinforcement; Mondale used a party concept, continuing to rely on old themes and old Democratic grassroots politics.

Using the marketing knowledge his team had gained from the 1980 campaign, Reagan won in 1984 by convincing the American electorate that America was strong and great. The Reagan campaign organization of 1984 continued to use the talents of sophisticated marketing experts in their packaging of Reagan, relying on simple themes of patriotism and family and, again, extensive negative advertising. Television ads such as his "Morning in America" commercial depicted flag-waving, happy, patriotic Americans. The reelection theme song was *I'm Proud to Be an American, Where at Least I Know I'm Free*. The theme was based on a brand reinforcement strategy, where the marketer attempts to hold onto its already loyal following, similar to what, for example, Dial soap does when its marketer uses the jingle, "Aren't you glad you use Dial?" The Democrats, on the other hand, tried unsuccessfully to create a feeling of discomfort by arguing that the budget deficit was too high and that the religious right was a threat to the country. Their scare tactics were not enough, and the Republicans won handily.

The success of Reagan in 1984 was due mainly to the image manufactured for him by his handlers, an image of a likable person who successfully combined a confident personality, excellent communication skills, and a strong commitment to religion and family.

AN OLD FORMULA WORKS AGAIN

In 1988, George Bush, using the same formula that Reagan finely tuned during his two terms in office, relied on negative advertising to label and define his opponent, Michael Dukakis. When Dukakis refused to fight back, his competition branded him as weak and unpresidential in the marketplace, and Dukakis lost. The most damaging ad by Bush was the infamous "Willie Horton" commercial. This 60-second spot showed Horton, a convicted criminal who committed another crime after Dukakis released him from prison early, walking through a revolving door. This ad reflected the state of the art of negative campaigning in the country at the time, which was used perhaps even more aggressively by Bush than by Reagan to destroy his opponent.

The Horton commercial drove Dukakis's negative ratings in the polls higher and effectively undermined the Democrats' claim to be the party of caring and compassion. The commercial ended with the sarcastic claim that Dukakis wants to do for America what he has done for Massachusetts. The Horton commercial continually reinforced the Republican mantra for 1988, which was to tell the American people that Bush offered them steady and tested leadership.

Dukakis's slogans, on the other hand, shifted from week to week. Many of Dukakis's commercials closed with the claim that the Bush people would like to sell the American people a package. Dukakis countered by saying that he was offering the American people the choice of a president, not a package, implying that Bush was being marketed to the American people in a slick manner. The Dukakis campaign was correct but failed in its attempt to convince the American electorate that it was being manipulated by marketing. The 1988 campaign was won, in large part, as a result of Bush's clever use of negative advertising, to which Dukakis never responded.

The success of the Bush campaign was based, in large part, on his control of the media and the issues from the Republican Convention through Election Day. Compared to Dukakis's commercials, Bush's commercials were consistent and tied in nicely to his debate performance. Dukakis spent much of the campaign trying to counter Bush's claims, evidence that Bush was successful in setting the agenda.

Bush also dominated the positive side of the airwaves, playing the role of the parent and grandparent with ads depicting him as a proud grandfather. Segments from Reagan's 1984 "Morning in America" commercials could be found in the Bush convention film and election eve program. Other Bush commercials played on those 1984 themes such as recapturing the small-town atmosphere in America.

THE NEW ERA

It was truly a new era in politics in 1992. This was a different type of election, with candidates circumventing the traditional communication links with voters and making direct contact through live talk shows. Ross Perot even announced his candidacy on television on *Larry King Live.* Bush continued to use his tried-and-true marketing platform, but Perot and Bill Clinton had caught on and made some marketing leaps of their own.

The 1992 campaign introduced American voters to the "war room," a high-tech nerve center that the Clinton organization used to monitor and direct all political communications. Set up in Little Rock, Arkansas, it housed computers, fax machines, and telecommunications equipment used to send out messages to every news station in the country almost instantaneously to combat the barrage of negative information being directed at Clinton. A sign that hung in the war room read "It's the Economy, Stupid," always reminding staffers and

Clinton to reinforce that theme. By doing this, he turned the focus from his character, on which Bush tried to center, to the economy and health care. The Clinton organization would not let Bush do to Clinton what he had done to Dukakis; every negative attack by Bush was countered immediately.

During the 1992 campaign, Democratic campaign strategists discovered that 40% of the American voters did not like either Bill or his wife, Hillary. In what was called the "General Election Project," they created a new image of the couple as well as the thematic messages Clinton would deliver. The key message centered on how Clinton was a change agent for the middle class who would stand up to the special interest groups out to hurt people in that group. The project spelled out the tactics used to drive home this theme: the plan called for building an image of Clinton as a child whose father died before he was born and who had struggled against an alcoholic stepfather who abused his brother and mother.[6]

The 1992 campaign was the first presidential election in which the traditional media were practically bypassed. Candidates appeared on unconventional, live call-in television shows, responding to voters who wanted to feel empowered and in touch with the men who would lead the free world for the next 4 years. Voters wanted their government back, and they voted for the candidate who represented this change. The ultimate effect was a change in perception by the American public of the candidates from political candidates to celebrities.

In 1992, candidates entered the living rooms of ordinary voters directly through cable television. Cable reached into more than 60% of television households, whereas the big three networks (ABC, NBC, and CBS) were losing their audiences. Clinton astutely responded by giving the voters what they wanted—direct access to the candidates. Clinton held televised town meeting shows in many states, honing the live debate skills that would serve him well in the October presidential debates.

Perot brought more changes in the 1992 campaign. Perot ran the first telemarketing campaign by a presidential candidate, and we came close to electing a man no one really knew. Through the sheer power of his personality—and $100 million—Perot gave the other "party-loyal" candidates a run for their money. Perot chose to appear before the American people not by going to rallies but rather by appearing on infomercials and distributing videocassettes, as well as campaign buttons and stickers, to voters. By relying on "800" and "900" telephone numbers to solicit money and volunteers, he actually tapped into a somewhat forgotten political tradition of creating a grassroots campaign organization.[7] The 1992 presidential campaign represented another major milestone in the continuing influence of marketing on politics and is captured in the book *The Marketing of the President*.[8]

DEJA VU ALL OVER AGAIN

In 1996, there was more of the same from the 1992 campaign. However, the key difference lay with the advantage of campaigning from the White House the second time around. Furthermore, the White House proved to be an effective fund-raising base for the presidents' strategists, making it possible for them to attract the kind of money that would allow them to market the president effectively. Another difference between 1992 and 1996 was the connection that Clinton made with the voters. From a marketing standpoint, Clinton was the "pet rock" candidate in 1992, the first baby boomer to run for the presidency. The president was a curiosity factor, someone who was different enough and a strong enough contrast to Bush to stand out from the crowd. In 1992, from a competitive standpoint, the president had his hands full.

In 1996, however, the president campaigned on a platform that was bigger than him personally. Clinton used one of the most effective marketing techniques, which was to offer to the American people something they truly needed. The product in 1992 was Clinton himself, but in 1996, the product was the message—the possibility of making the "American Dream" a reality for the children of voters, or what Clinton called the "age of opportunity."

Clinton won the presidency twice because he had the best marketing campaign. He was successful because he sent a message to the American people that matched their expectations and communicated it effectively to the American electorate. Clinton had the discipline to stay on his message throughout each of his two presidential campaigns and to stick to one theme during each campaign. During both of his campaigns, Clinton promoted himself as a "New Democrat" advocating social liberalism and economic conservatism and proclaiming significant changes for the country. A similar expression was used very successfully by Tony Blair in his successful bid to become prime minister in the United Kingdom when he relabeled himself the leader of "New Labour." As with Clinton, Blair's strategy worked. One of the major mistakes that then Prime Minister John Major made during his campaign against Blair was to agree to hold debates. This was the first time—and a sign of the "Americanization" of British politics—that candidates running for this position agreed to hold debates with one another.[9]

The American people have a very strong appetite for change, whether it is the new models that the automobile manufacturers put out each year or the latest fashions in women's clothing. Innovation in the political marketplace is no different from innovation in the commercial marketplace. Without innovation, a company, politician, or political party is doomed.

Clinton relied on the skills that one would find in modern-day marketing departments in corporations—competitiveness, flexibility, vision, and a willingness to rely on the most sophisticated technologies to market himself. He relied on focus groups and polls to direct his campaign strategy, which circumvented the media and went directly to the voters. Perhaps more than any other single issue, it was Clinton's ability to follow a market orientation, which centers a campaign on voters' concerns and desires rather than on his own, that enabled his message to get across as effectively as it did. A majority of the American electorate bought into Clinton's vision for America.

THE CAMPAIGN CHANGES

As we review recent presidential elections, it is apparent that the campaigns have become more direct and more mean-spirited. Negative ads, muckraking, and the delving media have combined with telemarketing, electronic electioneering, and electronic town hall meetings to produce a political climate so intimate as to be uncomfortable.

To the average voter, the first clue that it was not politics as usual was the excessive reliance on negative advertising during the 1988 campaign. This became especially apparent with the Horton ad by Bush against Dukakis.

A second indication that politics in this country is changing has been the unusually heavy reliance on polls. Polls overdramatize every speech a candidate makes, creating a "horse race" mentality in the election. During the 1992 and 1996 elections, hardly a news broadcast went by without a mention of the latest results from a new poll.

A third change has been the conspicuous reliance on handlers and "spin doctors," or paid consultants who coach the candidate on what to say and how, when, and where to say it. In some cases, the hired guns even reinterpret what the candidate just said to keep the candidate's image intact. It has become obvious to many voters that the candidates are highly programmed. What has not been as obvious is that the programming is based on the use of sophisticated marketing tools and techniques, the same ones used to market products and services.

A fourth big change came in 1992, with the first telemarketing campaign. Perot, instead of making campaign appearances like most presidential candidates, relied on television commercials, videocassettes sent directly to voters, and infomercials to get his message out. In addition, using recent advances in the telecommunications industry, he used television to solicit a volunteer network and campaign contributions. Just look at some of the highlights from the television era in politics during the last half of the 20th century[10]:

1952: There is extensive television coverage of the conventions.

1956: A total of $2.5 million is spent by both parties on television.

1960: A total of 17 million viewers tune into the Democratic Convention, with 8 out of 10 households watching the conventions. Kennedy and Nixon engage in the first televised debate.

1964: A total of 41 million people watch a color convention program on WGN. Lyndon Johnson introduces the country to negative advertising.

1968: Members of Congress make up their faces for television appearances.

1972: Nixon choreographs applause for his television appearance.

1976: Broadcasters spend $25 million on the Democratic Convention.

1980: More than 600 television support staff members cover each convention.

1984: Red, white, and blue balloons drop from the ceiling of the conventions.

1988: CNN covers its first convention.

1992: The big three networks average only a 5.8 share in the ratings, as fewer than 4 out of 10 households watch the conventions.

1996: Dan Rather of CBS leaves a convention before it is over.

AMERICAN POLITICS IN THE NEW MILLENNIUM

We have entered a new era in American politics, one that is being shaped by advances in telecommunications and information technology. Presidents before Clinton attempted to succeed at the same challenge that every leader has—to shape public opinion and attempt to persuade Americans to follow one's lead. Every president has tried to use the "bully pulpit" of the White House to shape people's thinking. However, we see technological advances taking place so quickly that it is truly changing the way in which the government is run, and it calls for a reengineering starting with a marketing orientation in the White House. To be successful, a president cannot afford not to understand how to use marketing in the White House.

American presidents in the new millennium will be faced with the same challenges that U.S. automobile manufacturers faced during the previous decade. Japanese competitors were entering the marketplace with better built, less expensive cars, forcing U.S. car manufacturers to develop new products that would be competitive. For example, Chrysler came out with the "minivan," which has been very successful. Similarly, future presidents will have to keep pace with advances in marketing technology to compete effectively.

At a forum on reinventing government, Vice President Al Gore spoke about the challenges that faced future political leaders. The language that Gore used could just as well have come from a corporate chief executive officer talking about changes being made in his or her organization. According to Gore, "In the long run, we have to build agencies—and, I might add, a congressional committee structure—that work more on horizontal than vertical lines. Partnerships and fluid organizations are the key because networks—not hierarchies—define government in the 21st century." Gore went on to say, "This means working across agency boundaries—blurring them into virtual organizations where the customer doesn't have to care which agency is actually delivering the service." The reference to the citizen as a "customer" of government services suggests that the vice president has every intention of borrowing technological advances from corporations as politics moves from a party orientation to a market orientation.[11]

CONCLUSION

The dilemma that politicians face today is that through the information technology that exists, citizens hear every utterance of a politician, and nothing can be said without the possibility of it getting into the news the next day. Furthermore, through the advent of talk radio and constant polling, politicians always know what is on the minds of the electorate. If they do not respond to the opinions of Rush Limbaugh and the polls, then they are thrown out of office. On the other hand, if they are too responsive and thus are seen as pandering (as Clinton has been portrayed), then they are criticized for being reactionary.

The proportion of Americans who trust their leaders has plummeted from 70% during the 1960s to approximately 20% today.[12] It could be a reaction to the alienation fostered by the talk radio movement. Or, it might be a reaction to politicians who refuse to stand up and go against the polls if they feel strongly about an issue. But most likely, it is in response to a political system that has lost control of what it is doing and reflective of a loss of power of the political party.

Since the procedural reforms of the mid-1970s and the expansion of the primary system, investigative reporters have been expected to inspect the candidates' platforms for the voters. The fact remains that it is much easier to get a negative message through the media than a positive one. This will continue to make it very difficult for presidents to be successful in the White House.

At the core of our problem as a democracy is the declining power of the political party and an American electorate that is simply fed up with the Washington politicians. Voters want people who are not political, even though most government processes are political. What is alarming about today's high-tech political system is the swiftness of the change taking place. It has become a way of life for voters.

NOTES

1. Jones, T. (1996, May 5). Conventional challenge. *Chicago Tribune,* sec. 1, pp. 1-2.

2. White, T. (1961). *The making of the president.* New York. Atheneum House.

3. McGinniss, J. (1968). *The selling of the president.* New York: Trident.

4. Krauthammer, C. (1995a, January 6). GOP's agenda should include restoring presidential powers. *Chicago Tribune,* sec. 1, p. 23.

5. Pika, J. A., Mosley, Z., & Watson, R. A. (1992). *The presidential contest: With a guide to the 1992 presidential race.* Washington, DC: Congressional Quarterly.

6. Friedman, T. L. (1992, November 12). Clinton to open military's ranks to homosexuals. *New York Times,* pp. A1, A9.

7. Newman, Bruce I. (1993, June). The role of marketing in the 1992 U.S. presidential election: How Bill Clinton was transformed from "Slick Willie" to "Mr. President." *Werbeforschung & Praxis,* pp. 195-201.

8. Newman, B. I. (1994). *The marketing of the president: Political marketing as campaign strategy.* Thousand Oaks, CA: Sage.

9. Mosley, R. (1997, March 18). British race to have an American accent. *Chicago Tribune,* sec. 1, p. 3.

10. See Jones (Note 1).

11. Dionne, E. J., Jr. (1998b, April 29). Reinventing government so that it's useful. *Chicago Tribune,* sec. 1, p. 19.

12. Ingalls, Z. (1993, April 28). Oklahoma archive of 50,000 radio and television commercials for political campaigns. *Chronicle of Higher Education,* sec. B4, p. 1.

3

The ABC's of Marketing

Repetition does not transform a lie into a truth.
—Franklin D. Roosevelt, radio address, October 26, 1939

When most people think of marketing, they think of advertising and promotion—McDonald's, Nike, and IBM. For years, politicians have relied on basic marketing skills—campaign buttons, posters, political rallies, and campaign speeches—to familiarize voters with a name, a party, and a platform. Abraham Lincoln used campaign buttons, posters, newspaper advertisements, and stump speeches—state of the art in marketing campaigns for politics at that time. Going back to Franklin D. Roosevelt, all modern-day presidents have relied on marketing to a greater or lesser degree to communicate their messages to the American people.

The same principles that operate in the commercial marketplace hold true in the political marketplace: Successful companies have a market orientation and are constantly engaged in creating value for their customers. In other words, marketers must anticipate their customers' needs and then constantly develop innovative products and services to keep their customers satisfied. Politicians have a similar orientation and are constantly trying to create value for their constituents by improving the quality of life and creating the most benefit at the smallest cost.

Every major corporation has a marketing department. For example, consider the Hershey Foods Corporation, which sells chocolate bars, Hershey kisses, Reese's candy, and other items. The marketing department for Hershey products includes sales representatives, marketing researchers, advertising specialists, direct marketing experts, and others. This department is responsible for developing marketing plans for each of the existing products and brands as well as developing new products and brands. People buy Hershey products because the company has an excellent reputation in the marketplace as selling a consistently good-tasting candy. Without marketing, Hershey's chocolate probably would be just as tasty, but few of us would know it, and the company probably would not be doing $1.8 billion in annual sales.[1]

A politician also sells something—ideas. More important, the politician is selling himself or herself to the American people and trying to convince them to buy into his or her vision for America. Each of the politician's ideas is formulated into programs that he or she must market to the American people. The candidate then enlists the help of several marketing professionals to convince Americans to vote for him or her.

Today, similar to the business world, it takes a good marketing researcher, media strategist, and direct mail specialist, as well as a stable of consultants and a lot of money, to win in politics. Many journalists have referred to this in newspaper and magazine articles as "retail politics," a reference to the person-to-person contact politicians make when they go out and "press the flesh" from dawn until dusk 7 days a week. Although the connection between the two markets is amazingly similar, it still is different in some significant ways.

MAKING THE LEAP FROM BUSINESS TO POLITICS

There are two glaring differences between the use of marketing in business and the use of marketing in politics. First, there are differences of philosophy. In business, the goal is to make a profit, whereas in politics, the goal is the successful operation of democracy (at least in this country). Winning in politics sometimes is based on a few percentage points, whereas the difference between winning and losing in business is based on huge variations. Second, in business, the implementation of marketing research results often is followed, whereas in politics, the candidate's own political philosophy can influence the extent to which it is followed.

The differences between business and politics have not prevented the practitioners of both areas from working to merge the two markets together. As a result, there are strong similarities between the two markets. First, both rely on the use of standard marketing tools and strategies such as marketing research, market segmentation, targeting, positioning, strategy development, and implementation (all of which are explained later in this chapter). Second, the voter can be analyzed as a consumer in the political marketplace, using the same models and theories in marketing that are used to study consumers in the commercial marketplace. Third, both are dealing in competitive marketplaces and, as such, need to rely on similar approaches to winning.

THE VOTER AS A CONSUMER

Marketers work very hard at shaping the expectations of their customers. Expectations of customers often are influenced by the gaps in thinking that exist between their own perceptions and those of the service provider. For example, Microsoft would like all computer users to think that they need to constantly upgrade their computers with the company's newest software products when they come out. Computer users, on the other hand, might not think that it is worth it to them to pay hundreds of dollars for these upgrades if they are able to continue to operate their computers without the new software. Voters experience similar gaps in politics[2]:

1. One gap exists between the expectation of consumers and management's perceptions of those expectations. For example, some airlines have gone out of business because they failed to keep prices down and services consistency high, an expectation of passengers that was not met. In politics, this might be difficult to measure because candidates shape their perceptions of the electorate after pollsters have told them what their constituencies expect. In other words, we have a case of the chicken and the egg. Particularly during presidential primaries, candidates often change policies and promises to align themselves with each state's electorate, even though their congressional voting records suggest different opinions altogether.

2. A second gap exists between quality specifications and service delivery. In other words, there might be constraints that prohibit candidates from delivering what they perceive to be of vital importance to the voters. For example, candidates might realize that voters in their constituencies have complaints about services rendered but might be incapable of delivering those services. Politicians are much more vulnerable to this gap than are other service industries as a result of the unexpected situations to which politicians always must respond.

3. There also exists a gap between management perceptions and service quality specifications. For example, when McDonald's Corporation decided in early 1998 to institute a new campaign to customize food orders because of its perception of the need for this in the marketplace, a very different challenge that faced the company was getting the franchisees to adopt the new service specifications. Situational influences (e.g., the House of Representatives shifting from a Democratic to a Republican majority as it did in 1994) make it difficult for a sitting president to set agendas that are responsive to citizens'

needs. In addition, as opposed to other service industries, politicians do not always have complete control over staffing because civil servants often are in positions not affected by changes in elected officials.

4. Finally, a fourth gap exists between the service delivery and external communications. In other words, promises made in advertisements and commercials that do not materialize in tangible results create problems for the service provider. This is especially important for the politician who often campaigns on platforms of promises that do not materialize into policy when he or she gets into office because of the bureaucracy in government or puffery on the part of the candidate as a means of getting into office.

THE POLITICIAN'S UNIQUE SERVICE OBLIGATIONS

There are three situations that set politicians apart from other service providers such as doctors and lawyers.[3] First, politicians are faced with situations that are both controllable and uncontrollable. In contrast to other service providers, politicians must react constantly to forces within the environment that are difficult to control. For example, when campaigning for office, there might be events that a candidate did not expect to happen such as a stock market crash, a military invasion, the death of another politician, and an accusations by a rival candidate. These events are uncontrollable by the candidate and can only be dealt with by having an organization that is flexible enough to respond. The politician can, however, control the course of events by establishing policies that are proactive rather than reactive.

A second dimension that sets politicians apart from other service providers is the dual roles played by politicians as both campaigners and policymakers. As campaigners, politicians are in the business of trying to win enough votes to get put into office. Careful scrutiny of their constituencies and competition is necessary to identify voter needs and to capture competitive niches in the marketplace. This often calls for the use of volunteers who are hired on a temporary basis to carry out grassroots activities. As policymakers, politicians rely on permanent staff who help them carry out their functions. The critical point to be made here is that the range of activities and resultant strategies very much depend on the roles that the politicians are playing.

The third distinction lies with the type and level of communication used by politicians and their organizations. Unlike other service providers, politicians rarely can meet in person with all of their customers (i.e., the electorate) and, instead, must rely on the use of mass media communications, public appearances, and direct mail procedures to make contact with their constituencies. In many cases, the politician's organization is responsible for making the contact. However, with respect to competition, the politician usually has more face-to-face contact than we find in most other service industries. One rarely sees doctors in head-to-head televised debates on who provides better service.

MARKETING AS AN EXCHANGE PROCESS

Marketing often is described as an exchange process between a buyer and a seller, with the buyer exchanging money for the seller's product or service. When applying marketing to a political campaign, the exchange process centers on a candidate who offers political leadership (through the policies he or she advocates) and a vision for the country in exchange for votes from the citizens. Once in office, particularly in the White House, the exchange centers on the same leadership and vision being offered to the American people in exchange for their votes of confidence (as measured through opinion polls that track the president's approval ratings). A president's leadership can be effective only if he is able to move legislation through Congress. However, as a president's approval ratings increase in the polls, there is an indirect pressure on congress-persons and senators to work with the president to avoid alienating their constituencies. Eventually, the exchange between a president and the American people moves to the next campaign, when the president runs for reelection. A market orientation then requires that research and polling be done to help shape the policies of the politician, which become the product through which the exchange is consummated.

MARKETING DECISIONS AND RESEARCH

At the core of marketing is the belief that extensive research must be carried out to determine the needs and wants of the marketplace before a product or service is developed. Similarly, marketing research is used by political leaders to shape policy. Bill Clinton and presidents before him have relied extensively on opinion polls to help determine the direction of their presidencies. Programs and policies are fine-tuned by first conducting focus groups and then using marketing research to develop tactics and strategies to frame the issues before they are presented in public. This process dates back to the early 1800s, when more primitive applications of these methods were used in campaigns.

As early as the 1820s, it was not uncommon to have interviews printed in newspapers as preelection "straw polls" (a term that came from the strong farming industry at the time in this country that revealed "how the wind was blowing"). The straw polls proved to be good circulation builders, and by the end of the 19th century, most major newspapers around the country were using them.

George Gallup introduced the world to polling in his Ph.D. dissertation that studied the newspaper reading habits of people. He determined that people read only about 15% of a newspaper. He also determined that men and women responded mainly to magazine advertisements that centered on sex appeal and product quality, a surprise to many executives who at the time were convinced that it was convenience and price that sold most products.

The introduction of sophisticated polling technology goes back to the mid-1930s, when Gallup introduced the concept when he was working at Young & Rubicam. At the time, the opinions of Americans were used by advertisers to determine how and where to place their advertisements. Gallup provided that information for both advertisers and politicians. What has become standard practice today was quite revolutionary when Gallup introduced it back during the 1930s. Gallup's first poll came in 1932, when he accurately predicted that his mother-in-law, Olga Babcock Miller, would win the race for secretary of state in Iowa. Using a carefully selected sample and the same techniques he used to study newspaper readership habits, Gallup invented the political poll. Immediately after that invention, Gallup teamed up with Harold A. Anderson, a Chicago newspaper agent, and founded a company that produced a newspaper column that was syndicated to newspapers around the country.[4]

There has been a general shift in recent years from reliance on polls to predict voters' behavior to the use of marketing research to provide explanations behind the predictions. In politics, opinion polls (called marketing research in the business world) have become one of the most important tools of the modern leader. In the commercial marketplace, marketing research is used to identify the needs and wants of consumers. The same techniques used to analyze why consumers buy a particular brand of soda or use the services of one health care provider over another are used by politicians to determine why voters prefer them over competing candidates. Since Jimmy Carter's campaign in 1976, candidates have relied extensively on marketing research to direct their campaign strategies.

The focus group is one specific marketing research technique that corporations have used for decades to test out new product concepts and advertising appeals. These are small groups of people, anywhere from 5 to 15 in number, who sit around a table and respond to questions directed at them by the focus group leader. People are chosen carefully for these sessions, usually recruited over the telephone, and are paid from $35 to $150 to participate. This technique is used during a political campaign to identify issues important to a segment of voters. In 1988, George Bush's pollster, Bob Teeter, ran a focus group with voters loyal to Michael Dukakis and found out that the one issue that they were sensitive to was the perception that Dukakis was soft on crime. The "Willie Horton" commercial was conceived based on this information.

There are many ways in which to artificially color the perceptions of voters to ensure victory at the polls. One of the tools that has become popular is called the "push poll." This is a deceptive political tool that uses a phone bank to call thousands of voters with questions that smear or denigrate the opposing candidate. For example, a question in this type of poll might be, "If you knew that Candidate X spent time in prison, would you still vote for him?"

Another way in which to color the perceptions of voters is to use 900 telephone number polls that measure the opinions of only those people who choose to call in and respond to the poll. Such polls are not random and, therefore, result in biased samples. Some candidates allegedly have used phone banks to swamp the lines with their supporters to sway the opinion that is reported.

One of the prerequisites to running a successful political campaign these days is the incorporation of opposition research into a candidate's campaign organization. The people who carry out this work are called in to find out anything they can on a candidate's opponents. Unfortunately, these people often are used to dig up dirt that eventually finds its way into political spots on television or radio or as leaks to the press. This is not a new activity. Opponents to early presidential contenders such as Thomas Jefferson and Grover Cleveland accused them of fathering illegitimate children.

According to the company listings in *Campaigns & Elections,* a political consulting periodical, there are well over 50 firms ready to hire out for opposition research work. Believe it or not, it is not unusual for a candidate to hire a firm to audit his or her own personal past looking for any vulnerable spots that might need to be protected. Here, the goal is to anticipate upfront what a rival might say about a candidate.[5]

The importance of doing research rests with the notion that not all products can be sold to all consumers. Companies use marketing research to determine what to stress to different consumer groups. Take the case of a cruise ship seeking to build its clientele. People who take cruises fall into different demographic groups. Some are older couples with no children looking for a relaxing vacation, whereas others are parents with children looking for a cruise with activities all day long to keep the kids occupied. Whether it is determining which movies to play on board, the choice of a menu, or even the type of pool activities to promote, cruise ships conduct marketing research to determine how best to satisfy the needs of each of these two key groups of customers. Politicians are no different.

For example, Clinton's choice of pushing for a bill to protect gays in the military at the start of his presidency was a strange decision. It alienated so many different interest groups that he had to retreat from the promise he made on that issue during the campaign. Herein lies the dilemma facing political leaders, who want to be responsive to the needs and desires of the citizenry. Even though leaders strongly believe in pushing through certain legislation, the cost to them in their approval ratings might be so great that they simply retreat from their positions.

During a political campaign, promises are made and then tested in the marketplace, something that is referred to as a "test market." Test markets usually are carried out in specific cities where the demographic profile resembles the rest of the nation. Peoria, Illinois, is one such city. A test market is one way in which McDonald's introduces new products. Prior to national distribution of the product, McDonald's offers its new product in selected restaurants and monitors customer demand and satisfaction. In effect, the test market is a simulated marketplace that serves as a forecast of consumer behavior.

Presidential candidates use this same procedure throughout the prenomination period, using primaries as a testing ground to arrive at a platform that encompasses the ideas and images that will be marketed from the convention onward. This, of course, changes from one election to the next.

Relying too heavily on polls can give way to an unprincipled acquiescence to public opinion. This is something that Bush found out ("Read my lips, no new taxes"). During the 1992 campaign, Clinton promised to be different.[6] In fact, Clinton, the good marketer that he was during his two presidential campaigns, promised the American people that he would not let the whims of public sentiment determine his policies. However, if we believe the account that Dick Morris wrote in his book, *Behind the Oval Office,* then the president not only has relied on polling extensively to determine and frame policy but has been intimately involved in questionnaire design and implementation.[7]

Like other Republican activists, Fred Steeper, one of Bush's pollsters, believes that some of Clinton's most popular and more moderate policies have been driven by surveys and focus groups. "Things like a [2]-year limit on welfare and three-strikes-and-you're-out on crime, we're all picking those up in our research. . . . Because the country is still of a conservative bent, the Clinton administration is finding our [Republican] agendas and trying to take them away."[8]

But voter opinions are getting more and more fickle these days. No longer is it a given that a person will respond to a poll when called. People are refusing to participate, thereby increasing the refusal rate and validity of polls. The current estimate for refusal rates by voters is very similar to refusal rates by consumers, that is, about 36%. This is a 12 percentage point increase over 1986, according to Walker Research, a firm based in Indianapolis, Indiana. Even when voters do cooperate, their answers are taken cautiously because of the strong skepticism that voters have about politics today.[9]

There is nothing wrong with the use of marketing research so long as a candidate or leader does not use the information to build an image-based campaign that makes promises that he or she knows never can be fulfilled. Unfortunately, candidates are building campaigns by crafting images of themselves that, in many cases, have no resemblance to either them or their ideas.

ANTICIPATING NEEDS

Success in marketing goes beyond the simple identification of the needs of consumers to include the ability to forecast what those needs will be in the future. Marketers not only must measure and identify the needs and wants of their customers but also must have a vision that enables them to anticipate what those needs will be. Whether it is a candidate, an issue, or a product, marketing is a critical component to understanding what voters, citizens, or consumers want and need. Needs may be driven by both emotion and rationality, resulting in people desiring the same product or candidate for different reasons.

Some people voted for Ronald Reagan in 1980 and 1984 because of his charisma, whereas others voted for him because they were convinced that he would strengthen the economy. Some people buy a car because it gets excellent gas mileage, whereas others buy the same car because it gives them a feeling of excitement and success when they sit behind the wheel. Whatever it is that is driving the behavior of people, marketing can be used to anticipate what their needs are and how one should go about marketing the product or service based on that information.

The most successful products are molded around the findings of needs assessment studies. Automobiles and gym shoes are just a few examples of product categories that follow a marketing orientation. The development of new car models and innovative gym shoes (e.g., pumps) was based on this type of research. Just as a smart marketer makes sure that there is a need for his or her product before the marketer distributes it around the country, so must a politician be sure that voters are concerned with an issue before the politician decides to advocate it.

Beginning with the primaries, candidates rely on needs assessment studies to determine how to present their ideas to the American people and to whom they should direct their advertising appeals. Primaries become opportunities to test out ideas, allowing candidates to test out new themes and issues as they move through the primary season to see what will sell with the voters.

Keep in mind that voters in different states have different needs and wants and look for different characteristics in a candidate. Voters in New Hampshire might have been more affected by the downturn in the economy during the 1992 election and, therefore, found Paul Tsongas more appealing because he was stressing economic issues in his platform. However, voters in the Midwest were not hurt by the ailing economy nearly as much as were those in the Northeast, resulting in primaries that had voters articulating a different set of needs and wants in the polls that were conducted. Candidates need to adjust their messages constantly, depending on their performances in the prior primary.

MARKET SEGMENTATION
AND TARGETING

Volvo has been selling its cars on the basis of safety features for years. The company realizes it has to appeal to car buyers with a unique offering that allows Volvo to make a good profit in the marketplace. The company has been an innovator in the structural design of car bodies to ensure the greatest safety possible for passengers. More recently, however, it has tried to alter its image by bringing in new models promoted on performance as well as safety. Who is the typical Volvo buyer? Market segmentation is a process that would be used to make that determination, and targeting is the selection of the segment(s) to which appeals are directed. This matches the buyer and seller, just as there has to be a match between a candidate and voter segments.

In business, market segmentation and targeting identify those groups of customers toward whom the marketer directs his or her product and promotional campaign. It is used by many companies that choose not to sell their products or services to every potential customer but rather only to those who are likely to buy it. 7-Up chose to be the "uncola" as a means of segmenting its market of potential soda drinkers who do not want to drink a cola. Avis adopted the motto "We try harder" to differentiate itself from the leading car rental company, Hertz, several years ago. Since then, companies such as Dollar and Budget entered the car rental market by offering lower prices (as their names suggest) as a means of segmenting their markets.

In politics, market segmentation traditionally has been used by each of the political parties to choose which segments of citizens it targets with its appeals. Historically, the Democrats have been the party of the poor and minorities, and the Republicans have been the party of the rich and big business. Each party worked hard at identifying the needs of its constituents and developing programs and policies geared at satisfying those needs. However, as the marketing technology has become available to tailor messages to meet the needs of all constituents, regardless of group identification, the segmentation of people along party lines has been blurred, with each party trying to attract citizens from the competing party. Remember the Reagan Democrats? These were Democrats who switched to Reagan in 1980 and 1984 and helped him to win both elections. This is the same segment of voters that Clinton successfully wooed back into the Democratic Party in 1992. In 1988, Bush effectively used a market segmentation strategy to differentiate himself from Dukakis by referring to Dukakis as a "liberal." By doing this, Bush was appealing to voters who wanted to support a "conservative" candidate. Clinton realized early in the 1992 campaign that one large market segment, the middle class, was ripe for targeting. The critical decision was finding the right message to appeal to this segment. Given the economic problems facing the country, Clinton decided to use various economic appeals such as the promise of more jobs and better wages.

POSITIONING

Positioning is the connection a company makes between its products and specific segments in the marketplace. To keep that connection alive, companies have to innovate constantly to maintain their leadership position. For example, in the personal computer industry, Apple first penetrated the market by targeting its innovative computers to customers looking to use them for educational purposes. IBM later followed with its version of the personal computer, opening up a new market geared to business. Apple then came out with the mouse, a device that defined the term "user-friendly." IBM soon followed. Along with the mouse came software that enabled users to work more easily with their personal computers. Positioning is critical to the success of any product, and it must incorporate changes and innovations on a regular basis to keep the product flourishing in the marketplace. The same holds true for politicians.

Once the multiple voter segments have been identified, the candidate has to position himself or herself in the marketplace. Positioning is a multistage process that begins with the candidate assessing both his or her own and the opponents' strengths and weaknesses. For example, in 1992, Clinton realized that, as a Democrat and an outsider to Washington, D.C., he was in a good position to criticize the system that Reagan and Bush had governed for close to 12 years.

In 1980, Reagan successfully positioned himself as the candidate who would fix the problems created by Carter. At the end of one of the campaign debates, Reagan asked voters the infamous question: Are you better off after 4 years of the Carter administration? It was a tactic that positioned Reagan as a leader with new ideas who would not resort to telling the American people that the country is in a malaise, as Carter did. Clinton positioned himself as a "New Democrat" in 1992, someone who would change the way in which Washington works.

IDEOLOGY AS A BRANDING MECHANISM

Every politician's reputation is perceived by people in the same way that products and services develop brand identities in the marketplace. The key difference is that a politician's reputation is intimately tied into his ideology. In marketing terms, ideology is a labeling process. People historically have used ideology as a way of labeling both themselves and politicians and then making a connection between themselves and the candidates (and the political parties to which the candidates belonged) through the use of this labeling.

These labels are no different from the ones we see on products or attached to services offered by a whole host of professionals who advertise in the hope of creating an image that defines who and what they stand for in the minds of consumers. Just look at what accountants did with H&R Block, what lawyers did with Hyatt legal services, or what Schwab did with financial services. Extensive advertising can be used to label and define who the provider is and what makes his or her services different from the competition. This is precisely what political parties and candidates do to sell their ideas to the American people.

Along with the constant shifting of people from one party to another has come a blurring of the definition of ideology in this country. However, instead of a majority of the people referring to themselves as liberals or conservatives, a majority of the people now refer to themselves as independents. (Forget about the ideological label called "moderate.")

Marketing has played a key role in reshaping political ideology in this country. Political ideology is being driven by marketing, not by party affiliation. In earlier presidential campaigns, ideology was based on fundamental differences in the way in which government was run. Today, the issues at the top of everyone's polls determine what leaders in both parties advocate. Presidential campaign themes such as "It's the Economy, Stupid" and "A Thousand Points of Light" are based on focus groups and polls. Likewise, the images manufactured for politicians are based on these same focus groups and polling results.

CONCLUSION

Moving public opinion in a desired direction is the marketing challenge to leaders in all democracies. Success in politics is measured by the ability of a leader to move public opinion in the direction he or she wants it to move. This is a short-term measure of success, but it also is the one barometer that everyone will look at on Election Day before the results come in.

It is critical for a president to know which part of the electorate to listen to and to which voters he should target his appeals. A serious issue to the health of our democracy is the ever-prevailing battle to do what is right for the country, even at the expense of losing popularity in the polls and possibly hurting the president's chances at getting reelected. Winning in presidential politics usually is measured by whether or not a president gets reelected (which equates to becoming a top-selling car in the automobile marketplace). However, winning as a country might have to come at the expense of a president's future.[10]

One of the best lessons that American marketers have learned in the past decade is that new product development has to be a continuous process, as the Japanese have shown us. Tom Peters, the management guru, suggests that a company should be producing at least a dozen new ideas each month on how to improve each of its product lines. The process is one whereby everyone in the company is constantly thinking of ways in which to make minor improvements to the products or services.

In a company, the scientists and engineers in the firm's research and development department must understand the needs of the users of their products. However, customers' needs change over time (as do the attitudes of citizens bombarded by information), and it is incumbent on the company to develop a process aimed at finding ways in which to continue to meet consumer needs.

Given the intense competition in most markets today, companies that fail to develop new products expose themselves to great risk. Existing products are vulnerable to changing consumer needs and tastes, new technologies, shortened product life cycles (the stages a product goes through from the time it is introduced to the time it is taken off the market), and increased competition. At the same time, new product development is risky. For example, Texas Instruments lost $660 million before pulling out of the home computer business, RCA lost $575 million on its failed videodisc players, Ford lost $350 million on its ill-fated Edsel, and Bob Dole lost the 1996 presidential election because of his failure to take the risk of changing in response to voter needs and wants in the marketplace. At the same time, political candidates will continue to win elections and succeed in office because they reposition their policies and images in response to the changing needs and wants of voters following the same marketing formula that works for corporations.

NOTES

1. Kotler, P. (1994). *Marketing management* (7th ed.). Englewood Cliffs, NJ: Prentice Hall.

2. Adapted from Parasuraman, A., Zeithaml, V. A., & Berry, L. L. (1985). A conceptual model of service quality and its implications for future research. *Journal of Marketing, 44.*

3. Newman, B. I. (1988). A services oriented strategic framework for politicians. In *Proceedings of the seventeenth annual Decision Science Institute Western Regional Conference* (pp. 192-195). Honolulu, HI: Decision Science Institute.

4. Smith, R. (1997, Winter). Letting America speak. *Audacity,* pp. 50-62.

5. Mosley, R. (1997, March 18). British race to have an American accent. *Chicago Tribune,* sec. 1, p. 3.

6. Carney, J. (1994, April 11). Playing the numbers from healthcare to Whitewater, the Clinton administration relies heavily on polling. *Time,* p. 40.

7. Morris, D. (1997). Behind the Oval Office: Winning the presidency in the nineties. New York: Random House.

8. See Carney (Note 6).

9. Landler, M. (1992, July 6). How good are polls? We refuse to answer. *Business Week,* pp. 29-30.

10. Peters, T. (1994, September 5). Asking me is not a solution: Do something. *Chicago Tribune,* sec. 4, p. 3.

4

The Information Highway

The reduction of politics to a spectator sport . . . has been one of the more malign accomplishments of television. Television newsmen are breathless on how the game is being played, largely silent on what the game is all about.

— John Kenneth Galbraith, *A Life in Our Times* (1981)

In 1920, Republican presidential candidate Warren G. Harding used a phonograph recording during his successful campaign. In 1944, Franklin D. Roosevelt used the radio with his "fireside chats" to successfully win election. The radio was the medium that Roosevelt used in his successful bid for a fourth term when he formally opened his campaign in an address to the Teamsters Union. In fact, the fireside chats became more than just a campaign tool; they became one of his most effective governing tools. Today, with the rise of the Internet and low-cost digital telecommunications, the traditional model of communication is fast becoming outdated. Most candidates running for public office have homepages on the World Wide Web. With some cheap software, a homepage can now be set up in about 15 minutes.

Throughout U.S. history, politicians have exploited the technology of the day, beginning with the printing press during the American Revolution that allowed wide dissemination of handbills. Later, railroad made travel more practical for candidates and spawned the "whistle stop" campaign of Harry Truman, copied by Bill Clinton during his successful reelection bid in 1996. Radio and television gave politics an instantaneous quality that computers are enhancing with the introduction of the Internet. It was not that long ago that political campaigns sent out news releases using bicycle messengers. Now,

49

facsimile machines are used to deliver messages in seconds, compressing the news cycle from days to hours—or even to minutes. Today, the Internet is being used by politicians and activists to reach millions of potential constituents through computer links on the Web. The Internet offers easy access to information about candidates today with the simple click of a button. Interested voters can see images and words come alive as the biography of a candidate sits right in front of them.[1]

Every time the president makes a stop, it takes 25 to 30 people to set up and operate the telephone system for the traveling White House. If the president goes on a trip lasting several days, then it takes some 300 people to set up the phone systems. On one trip that George Bush made overseas, 1,000 communications employees went along to set up the telecommunications links.[2]

The amazing technological revolution has altered both the commercial and political marketplaces through advances in telecommunications. These advances have made it possible for marketers to mass customize products, enabling them to mass produce while at the same time customizing products to the individual tastes and desires of one consumer or voter at a time. For example, computer companies such as Dell and Gateway 2000 enable customers to customize their systems and, at the same time, mass produce computers for millions of people. Likewise, politicians can target different messages to different constituents, depending on their interests and backgrounds.

Traditionally, political consultants have relied on four major media vehicles with paid advertising to communicate to voter segments: television, radio, newspapers, and magazines.[3] However, recent advances in telecommunications technology have given consultants the opportunity to target their messages far more effectively using other vehicles such as Internet Web pages, e-mail, and other forms of direct marketing. In fact, for politicians, the Internet offers a cost-effective way in which to talk directly to voters. There are no space limits, and the cost of posting 10,000 words is almost the same as that of posting 100 words. With close to $7 billion being spent by political advertisers during 1996, direct marketers certainly will be in stiff competition with executives of other media outlets to attract the large amount of money that is certain to be spent in upcoming campaigns.[4]

GATEKEEPERS ON THE INFORMATION
HIGHWAY: THE MEDIA

In a major study by the Center for Media and Public Affairs, it was concluded that all three presidential candidates in 1992 received far more bad press than good press, leaving one with the impression that the media are in part to blame for the nagging problem we have today with the distrust of officials in the nation's capital. In fact, since 1980, press coverage of all candidates has been more negative than positive. A generation ago, most Americans liked or admired the man they elected president. Lately, pollsters tell us that people regard their candidate as the lesser of two evils.

Political campaign organizations have had to rely on the media for decades to get their message out to the electorate. To the politician who wins an election and is sitting in office trying to govern, the role of the media becomes even more important. Journalists in the media have become the most important opinion leaders in the country for any politician, from a local candidate running for school board to the president looking to occupy the White House.

The media now have the job of reporting on any "dirt" that is dug up on a politician. The background checks on the character of candidates used to be carried out by party insiders, but this job has been passed on to the media. In their new omnipotent role, the media carry with them a tremendous responsibility. The stars at presidential conventions no longer are just the candidates and politicians but now include the television anchors. News has become entertainment in this country.[5] Ever since Gary Hart challenged the press to "catch him in the act," the line between the professional and personal lives of candidates has been crossed. When John F. Kennedy was president, the press never would have reported on any of his sexual liaisons. This is a far cry from the stories that have surrounded Clinton during his two terms in office. With the benefit of hindsight, even the Gennifer Flowers story now seems tame compared to the spate of sexual allegations that have arisen since the Monica Lewinsky story broke in January 1998.

In 1987, Ronald Reagan amended the Fair Doctrine Act, eliminating the regulation that required the media to give equal air time to both sides of an issue. Since then, talk radio has taken on a new, more powerful role in our democracy, and it is not about to stop anytime soon. Talk radio clearly is not a new phenomenon. It goes back to the Franklin D. Roosevelt presidency, when Father Caughlin, an advocate of extreme right-wing politics, took on a powerful position in the media as a talk radio show host. Talk radio is to political consumers of information what the Home Shopping Network is to some shoppers in the commercial marketplace, that is, a very convenient outlet to buy products.

The number of stations that devote part of their broadcasts to talk has more than tripled between 1990 and 1995, increasing from approximately 300 stations to close to 1,000 during this period. In large part, this is because advanced satellite technology reduced the cost to radio stations to simulcast radio shows around the country. Rush Limbaugh's radio program currently is simulcast over 600 stations around the country, reaching more than 20 million people daily. By getting placed in powerful media positions, people such as G. Gordon Liddy, Oliver North, and Mario Cuomo influence public opinion. Imagine the uproar if 20 years ago, a talk show host directed listeners to respond to police raids by

shooting for the groin and legs to avoid hitting the chest armor. This is what
Liddy, a former Watergate criminal, told his listeners soon after the Oklahoma
City bombing in 1995.

The media have turned into one of the new "party bosses" in U.S. politics.
Ever since investigative reporters Bob Woodward and Carl Bernstein blew open
the Watergate scandal, the media have taken on a more powerful role in
presidential politics. They have the power to turn an unknown candidate into a
celebrity, as they helped to do with Clinton in 1992, or ruin the candidacy of a
hopeful politician, as happened to Hart in 1988.

In the business marketplace, companies use opinion leaders to promote their
products and services. Sports figures, movie stars, and other highly visible
personalities are opinion leaders because consumers look to them for advice.
In the same vein, the media, and in particular network news anchors, serve as
opinion leaders for voters.

TRADITIONAL CHANNELS
OF COMMUNICATION

Each traditional major advertising medium becomes more or less important,
depending on the level of race and financial strength of the political party and
candidate. Furthermore, each medium plays a slightly different strategic role in
the overall promotional strategy of a candidate. Free political advertising is
available to all candidates and parties over each medium, depending on the
ingenuity of the candidate and his or her organization. As the level of the race
moves from a local to a national level, the media become more interested and
likely to follow a candidate from stop to stop. It is not uncommon for presidential candidates to organize a day's activities around stops that coincide with
prime-time dinner coverage on the local news station in critical localities.

As the level of a political race moves from a local to a national level,
television advertising becomes more important for two reasons. First, the reach
of the medium is greater and is necessitated by the greater number of people
who need to be reached over a short period of time. Second, national campaigns
(e.g., Congress, president) are better financed and, therefore, can absorb the
high cost of television advertising.

Television is used by presidential candidates and sitting presidents to broadcast town hall meetings, that is, gatherings of citizens who question the politicians. Clinton used this communication channel extensively during his two
presidential campaigns and at various points in his tenure to market various
programs to the American people. As a sitting president, the channel is used to
influence public opinion in an effort to pressure Congress to pass the president's
legislation. CNN, a major media outlet, also uses electronic town hall meetings
in a daily program called *Talk Back Live*. The program provides viewers with a

live audience, or town hall meeting format, that is a backdrop to experts as they are interviewed about various issues on the political agenda of the nation. This format likely will become a permanent fixture on many other television networks and stations.

Television also has been used by politicians to broadcast "infomercials," that is, crosses between commercials and paid programs. Used for many years by businesses touting everything from the latest remedy for baldness to time-saving ways in which to strip furniture, infomericals were popularized in politics by Ross Perot in his bid for the presidency in 1992 as a more cost-effective channel for him to get his message out to the American people. Similar to the electronic town hall meetings, infomercials give politicians an unfiltered communication link with the American people, allowing them to get their messages across without the contamination of journalists asking tough questions.

At a local level, where newspaper endorsements become critical issues for candidates, this medium is used much more extensively. Newspaper advertising also is quite a bit cheaper than other advertising outlets. Radio also is popular at a local level because it is less expensive, with a reach nearly as wide as television in some instances. Candidates often rely on the radio to deliver their most negative messages for two reasons. First, the message is more likely to penetrate with less resistance because of the nature of the medium. Most people are busy doing something else as they listen to the radio, making them less able to counterargue the points made against a candidate. Second, the sender of a negative message is not interested in being identified, which radio makes possible.

One of the more recent channels of communication that political campaigns have borrowed from business is direct marketing. The same technologies used to target direct mail to residences have been used since the mid-1970s to target fund-raising letters to voters and wealthy individuals. For example, during the 1992 and 1996 presidential campaigns, candidates used "800" telephone numbers to make direct links between themselves and the voters. Both Perot and Jerry Brown relied extensively on telemarketing efforts to solicit funds from supporters. This channel of communication has become more popular since the reforms of the 1970s, when limits were put on the amount of money that any one individual or organization can contribute to a candidate or political party. Before the 1970s, presidential candidates relied on wealthy donors to bankroll their campaigns, as Richard Nixon did with W. Clement Stone, the insurance tycoon.

Political organizations usually use direct marketing in an election if television is too expensive, if television is so cheap that the organization cannot spend all of its money on that medium alone and so adds direct mail to the mix, if the current media market is inefficient (e.g., a target district that is a small piece of a bigger market area), if the district straddles multiple media markets (i.e., one media market is efficient, but the district stretches into a second, less efficient, more expensive market), or if the organization needs to narrowcast a message (some messages, especially negative ones, are not as well suited to a broadcast audience).[6]

So, whereas the critical elements of campaign strategy have not changed dramatically over the past 30 years, the methods for achieving political goals have been changed substantially. Successful campaigns must develop a message that is focused on targeted groups of voters that will swing the election for the candidate. Furthermore, all campaigns share several communication goals including name identification of the candidate, candidate image, issue development, attack, and defense. This is where the media play such a critical role. The media, through both the paid and free information they communicate to the electorate, become the channels through which a candidate gets his or her message across to the voters. A major industry has evolved to assist the candidate in getting his or her message to the voters through the media. This has resulted in a significant political transformation of American political campaigns from a vehicle for grassroots movements to multimedia campaigns.[7]

A HI-TECH CHANNEL OF COMMUNICATION: THE INTERNET

In the past decade, the newest tool in the arsenal used by politicians trying to initiate change and get elected to public office is the Internet. The information highway is slowly moving the American voter from the "age of emotion" into the "age of reason." This movement is taking place as citizens begin to rely on the Internet instead of television as their source of political information. With the television came the ability to appeal to people's emotions through the visual and audio capabilities of the medium. With the onslaught of the Internet revolution, fancy peripherals are being replaced by access to tremendous amounts of information at the touch of a button, moving programming control from the broadcaster to the individual in the privacy of his or her household. This information highway will alter politics as we know it today.[8]

The Internet not only connects people to each other but also connects people to the equivalent of an on-line public library, where information about any topic can be retrieved on demand.[9,10] The coming digital millennium will give us the capability to work, shop, and entertain ourselves in a new on-line realm that will put every conceivable piece of information at our fingertips instantaneously.[11,12]

The first introduction of the Internet to the commercial marketplace came with the SABRE and Apollo airline reservations systems used by some major airlines to schedule flights. This soon expanded into a full-blown channel of communication today used by millions of people to get information and buy products and services. Technically speaking, the Internet is a highly decentralized network of computer networks that includes wide area networks (or WANs) and local area networks (or LANs). The Internet originated during the 1960s when the Department of Defense funded research that linked computer networks at the time that were incompatible. Out of this research emerged the World Wide Web, an Internet service that has become the avenue through which politicians and others communicate with people around the world.

The likelihood that the Internet is used by companies depends on the characteristics of the products and services being sold. For example, if it is a product or service, such as a television set that needs to be experienced before it is purchased, then the usefulness of the Internet will not be as great. On the other hand, if the product can be bought on the basis of objective characteristics, such as a magazine subscription, then the Internet will be more useful. When we examine politics from this perspective, it is clear that the Internet will not be as useful in its current stage of technological sophistication because it is difficult to view the candidate as one would on television, where there is an experience taking place. But as the medium becomes more advanced, there will be the opportunity to experience the candidate in the same way that we currently do on television.[13]

The most common forms of advertising on the Internet are homepages and interactive brochures, which some think will eventually replace the mass media as we know them. The Internet is in the process of being transformed into a broadcast medium that will have properties similar to television, with the exception that it will have a personalized characteristic making both programming and advertising customized to an individual's tastes and desires. This will be especially important to politicians, who will be able to provide a database of information for interested voters on subjects of concern only to certain people and not to others.[13]

There are three assumptions about the Internet that support the claim that it is a technological change that will alter the political landscape in the future. First, there will be near universal access to the Internet in the United States for both business and personal use. Second, the use of the Internet for marketing purposes will result in a redistribution of revenues among many different companies within a channel of distribution. Third, security while communicating on the Internet will be a critical issue, especially as it applies to the possibility of creating a more "user-friendly" way in which to vote. Currently, it is possible for someone using the Internet to be tracked by a company and then traced as he or she moves from one Web site to another. For politicians, this last assumption could be a very crucial issue if the medium is used for strategic interactive and marketing research purposes.[14]

As the Internet is transformed into a broadcast medium that has properties similar to those of television but with personalized characteristics making both programming and advertising customized to an individual's tastes and desires, politicians will move a step closer to being able to mass customize their images and ideas to targeted audiences. In the business world, this is referred to as "one-to-one" marketing between the company and an individual customer. In this system, the cost to get information about a product or politician is greatly reduced to both the sender of the information and the person seeking it.[14]

In an earlier chapter, we referred to marketing as an exchange process between the marketer (or politician) and the consumer (or voter). There are three channels through which this exchange may take place over the Internet: distribution channels, transaction channels, and communication channels. Distribution channels serve as the places where there is a physical exchange of products and services. On the product side, this would be the retail outlet where someone goes to purchase a product. On the political side, this would be any place where citizens and politicians meet to exchange information (e.g., a town hall meeting).

Transaction channels are places where sales activities between buyers and sellers take place without physical interaction. On the product side, this could be a catalog order or an interactive channel such as the Internet, where a sale is made without physically meeting. On the political side, this would be the polling booth where the voter casts his or her ballot for a particular politician.

Finally, communication channels create the opportunity for information to be exchanged between buyers and sellers. On the product side, this would be any medium such as the newspaper or a television commercial. The same would hold true for the politician, who also uses all of these channels to communicate with the voters. Given the efficiency and flexibility of the Internet, it likely will have its greatest impact in politics as a communication channel.[14]

For the first time during the 1996 presidential campaign, we heard one candidate, Bob Dole, actually give out his Web site address during a debate. The only problem was that the people who took down Dole's Web site address got nothing more than an error message because Dole gave out the wrong site location. "If you really want to get involved, just tap into my homepage, www.dolekemp96org," he said in his closing remarks. The problem was that he left out a crucial "dot" symbol in his address. Those people who followed Dole's directions received a "try again" message. Some even found themselves keying into the Clinton-Gore homepage in their attempt to find the Dole-Kemp homepage.

Dole's mention of the address during the debate was the single biggest advertisement for a Web site in history. Visitors to the site found biographies of Dole and Jack Kemp along with their campaign schedules and stances on issues, volunteer information, and a calculator that computed how much families would save under Dole's proposed 15% tax cut. In 1996, an estimated 25 million Americans had at least some access to the Internet, and more than 2 million used it on a regular basis. According to Lorena O'English of Project Vote Smart, which publishes a 244-page directory for political sites on the Internet, approximately 5% of all Americans used the Internet for information in the 1996 campaign.[15]

Newt Gingrich also jumped onto the Internet bandwagon with his new computer system that plugged people into the workings of Congress. This new congressional system makes it possible for citizens to search for legislation to give them an insight into the lawmaking process. This followed the lead set by the White House in October 1994 that brought government on-line.[16]

Another first happened during the 1996 Democrat Convention, where viewers could talk back directly to convention participants. With technology that will open up conventions on an interactive basis the way in which town hall meetings have done, voters communicated directly with delegates and even participated in delegation conferences in hotel meeting rooms through the aid of videoconferencing. The connection was made possible with the creation of a "hotlink" for convention news and messages on the City of Chicago's homepage on the Internet. The Web site enabled interested parties to hear about convention events and volunteer opportunities. In fact, applications for new volunteers were even posted on the site. At the convention, each state delegation was equipped with a personal computer on the floor of the convention hall.[17]

MOVEMENT TOWARD A CYBERDEMOCRACY

The Internet offers a very cost-effective way in which to talk directly to voters. For politicians, the Internet offers a new way in which to communicate directly with citizens. Access to the Internet is more or less open to all people interested. Some politicians like the idea that their constituents can use the Internet to contact them very efficiently and cost-effectively, giving them a necessary feedback loop to stay in touch with the people who put them into office. In 1995, Clinton was getting 1,000 to 2,000 e-mail messages a day. However, many politicians complain that close to 80% of the e-mail messages they get are from out of state because it only takes the click of a button for an irate citizen or an interest group to send a message to every member of Congress simultaneously.[18]

Each of the four traditional media used by politicians in the past has changed the nature of politics in its own way. The printing press made it possible for the mass circulation of newspapers and then magazines. Radio and television outlets made it possible for government leaders to speak directly to many people at one time in a far more intimate way than in public gatherings. In a similar way as the four traditional media have made their impact, so will direct marketing, especially as it is used through the Internet. In particular, the use of the Internet as a direct marketing tool is, in effect, a print medium communicated to people over a screen in a manner similar to how programming is carried by television. The use of the Internet by direct marketers presents a very unique combination of technologies that eventually will help it to become an integral part of every politician's marketing strategy. Voters might even be able to cast their ballots from computers in their homes in the future. Candidates will have the opportunity to make direct contact with voters with on-line debates that could be viewed in real time or on a time-elapsed basis.[19]

The serious presidential candidate today must have a homepage on the Web. In 1994, creating a homepage on the Web was regarded as cutting-edge technology. Today, the software is available for the average computer user with a few hundred dollars to create a homepage. As the voting public becomes more well connected to the Internet, the communication avenue will expand beyond the truly committed to the average citizen. Instead of watching television after dinner, the average citizen will "surf the Web." Because of the low cost of using the Web, all that a campaign has to do is find a volunteer with the required knowledge and put him or her to work sending out messages to interested parties. This has made Web pages attractive to politicians, especially those who are strapped for dollars but still want to find activists and recruit supporters. Believe it or not, the cost to set up a Web page could be as little as $100 to register the name for the first 2 years and then about $20 per month to maintain access to the page. Start-up costs can reach $200 if a candidate hires a computer specialist, and the monthly cost can go as high as $300 for a Web page that reports how many people look at it daily and where they live. When this is compared to other direct marketing techniques currently used by politicians, it is far more cost-effective. The costs of sending out mailings or setting up phone banks are much higher.[20]

The adaptation to the Internet by political consultants is not that easy. In the past, every communications revolution has increased the possibility of reaching a larger and more diverse audience. With the use of the Internet as a direct marketing tool, the challenge is slightly different and will present two serious difficulties.[21]

First, the Internet offers the user an unedited information base. It will be more difficult to trace the source of a direct marketing communication sent over the Internet. Let us not forget the enterprising young college student who, in the 1996 presidential campaign, created a *Bob Dole for President* Web page that looked like the real thing but was really designed to hurt the candidate. Newspapers, magazines, television, and radio stations all bundle their information with a clearly identifiable logo or station number to give an identity and credibility to the person and information conveyed. For those voters who want to have that "security" when they receive information over the Internet, the challenge will be great to the provider.

Second, the Internet is an interactive medium, a characteristic that should play into the hands of direct marketers, who are actively seeking ways in which to motivate the receivers of their messages to respond. However, this will put more pressure on the direct marketers using this medium to stay on top of the process 24 hours a day if they want to have personnel ready at all times to respond to the interested parties who want more information.

The Internet, the Web, and e-mail all have become commonplace tools used by politicians to target both voters and journalists with their messages. Only a few thousand computer researchers and academics even knew about the Web at the beginning of the 1990s. The Internet has moved computerized communication from its infancy in the 1992 campaign to a serious outlet that many candidates running for office at all levels are beginning to use.

For example, during the 1996 presidential election, each of the candidates had a homepage with information on his background and platform. In his coverage of the 1996 campaign, Brock Meeks, the chief correspondent in Washington, D.C., for *Wired* and *Hotwired,* used the presidential candidates' homepages to get faster access to their press releases than by going to a public relations newswire or the fax machine. Political Internet sites have become "first-stop shopping" for journalists and interested voters who are closely following movements in political campaigns. One needs only to go back to the breaking news of the Lewinsky scandal to know that the story broke on the homepage of the *Drudge Report,* an Internet site operated by Matt Drudge, who became a political hot potato overnight with his breaking news. Nearly every major newspaper, magazine, and television station now has a homepage on the Internet.[22]

In a survey carried out during the 1996 election cycle, the use of computers and on-line services among registered Democratic, Republican, and Independent voters was studied. Of those people surveyed, 41% of Democrats, 49% of Independents, and 50% of Republicans indicated that they owned computers. However, it was the Democrats who were most likely to use on-line services, with 21% saying that they used these services and only 15% of the Republicans and 19% of the Independents saying that they used them. The 35- to 49-year age group is the segment that both major parties have targeted, as members of this group are most likely to own computers. The Web sites used in the 1996 election on the part of both parties were geared to new and younger voters who would be less likely to receive their information from newspapers, television, and radio. There is, of course, the added benefit of appearing to be "high tech" by having a Web site.[23]

Doug Bailey, a former Republican political consultant and cofounder of the American Political Network, predicts that e-mail will become the most common method of political fund-raising, one of the most important reasons for politicians to use direct marketing methods. In 1996, Perot's United We Stand America Party relied on e-mail to keep the movement's adherents in touch with one another. Every on-line service has areas devoted to political discussions, a great way for politicians and journalists alike to keep track of what voters are saying about candidates and the issues for which they stand. The downside to this technology is that bulletin boards could become a way for negative material to be spread with no way to track down the sources of the messages.[24]

Adam Sohn, director of technology for the reelection of Clinton in 1996, estimated that the president's Web site generated 1 million "hits" during its first 10 days. A Dole campaign aide indicated that Dole's Web site had generated 9 million hits from September 1995 through August 1996. Furthermore, close to 6,000 Republican campaign volunteers signed up via the Web. At this point in time, the Internet is not a way in which to get around the mainstream press but rather a forum to allow candidates to articulate their messages. The Internet as a direct marketing tool enables interested parties to get information that would otherwise be obtained through the more traditional outlets such as television, newspapers, and magazines. If a candidate is able to get people on-line, then the candidate has the opportunity to shape his or her story directly, thereby eliminating the use of intermediaries possibly interfering with the message the candidate wants to get across to the people. What is most interesting is that a high percentage of the registered voters on the Web are "swing voters," that is, those not satisfied with either major party who are looking to make their votes count. If the candidates from the major parties can figure out how to use this medium to their advantage, then they stand to benefit tremendously.[25]

BREAKING THE LEWINSKY STORY
ON THE INFORMATION HIGHWAY

Even before the story surfaced on CNN and other major news networks concerning Clinton's alleged affair with a former White House intern, Lewinsky, the story was sent all over the world through the *Drudge Report*. Drudge, the editor of the report, has been accused of circulating false reports over the Internet. One such accusation resulted in an apology when he reported that Sidney Blumenthal, an adviser to Clinton, had been charged with spousal abuse, a story that Drudge had to admit was false. Just how does someone—almost anyone—who has Internet capabilities carry off such a feat?[26]

The rumor about Clinton was posted on Drudge's own Web page, something anyone can have created for him or her by a computer expert for a very nominal fee. A shorter version of the story also was posted through Drudge's America Online account to the 10 million subscribers to this Internet provider service. At the same time, he mailed the same rumor to thousands of subscribers to an e-mail mailing list. It did not take too long before several investigative reporters began to check out the story.

The story hit the Web late on a Saturday night after Drudge filed his report. Almost simultaneously, a well-known reporter for *Newsweek* magazine, Michael Isikoff, developed what many believed was the story of his career, only to have it stopped right before the magazine went to print. Early Sunday morning, someone posted the Drudge report on a Web site devoted to current events that deal with the Whitewater investigation. Later Sunday afternoon, the story was spread to a Web site devoted to discussion of impeachment of the president. Sunday morning, on the television program *This Week With Sam Donaldson and Cokie Roberts* on ABC News, William Kristol, editor of the *Weekly Standard* and a regular guest on the program, decided to insert the story onto the program. Kristol made the point that *Newsweek* was planning to run with the story based on tape-recorded conversations between the intern and a former White House staffer that were made available to Isikoff. Discussion then ensued on the television program between Kristol and Donaldson, who made the point that if *Newsweek* editors decided that they did not have enough information to run with the story, then he did not think it was proper to talk about it on the program. The conversation was quickly ended by Roberts.[27]

The story picked up steam later that day on CNBC's *Equal Time,* another television program devoted to politics. The discussants on the program agreed that Isikoff is a very good reporter, that *Newsweek* must have gotten cold feet, and that Drudge is merely a gossip reporter. On Monday morning, more reports were posted on the Web, with an update by the *Drudge Report* and the name of the White House intern. The report also reported on the "story behind the story," which was beginning to gain its own momentum. The exchange that took place on Sunday on the ABC News program was recanted on another Web site, *Pundit Central,* and was the featured story on *Webzine*'s "Underground." CNBC's *Rivera Live* and CBS Radio's *Mary Matalin Show* added fuel to the rumor fire. However, it was not until Wednesday morning that the *Washington Post* and *Los Angeles Times* decided to run with the story in their later home editions after withholding it from their earlier editions that day. It is of interest to note that when the story did come out in the later editions, there was no mention of the *Drudge Report.* On Wednesday, CNN and the wire services started airing updates of the story on the hour, with other television networks and major news Web sites (e.g., *CNN Interactive, MSNBC, ABCnews.com*) soon following.

This is one possible outcome to the use of the Internet, namely, the ability for anyone to send any message he or she wants and, in effect, to carry out an on-line town meeting. The White House intern scandal played itself out in this very manner, with interactive polls and message boards erected within hours to allow the public to voice its opinion. These discussions, called "newsgroups" on the Internet, created a real town hall environment. It was almost as if we had moved with this event into a new cyberage in which people became glued to their computers in the same way as people typically had been glued to their television sets. In fact, a *USA Today* spot survey drew close to 16,000 respondents in about a day's time. Similarly, the number of times that people called up *USA Today Online* went up dramatically over the course of the week when the story first broke.[28]

THE MERGING OF TRADITIONAL AND INTERNET NEWS

The way in which the Lewinsky story was reported might have blurred the lines across traditional and Internet news outlets to the point where the two never again will be separated. Millions of people at home and at work began to turn to the Internet to get the latest news about the alleged affair in the weeks that followed after the story broke. The ability of the Web to break news faster than traditional media outlets gives it a unique offering that will force the major news networks, newspapers, and magazines to tie their operations more intimately to the Internet.

Although it is difficult to make exact counts, there is substantial evidence that the traffic on Web sites increased as much as two- to threefold during the first few weeks after the story broke. The difficulty of determining exactly how many people use the Internet to get information from a Web site is that it is impossible to know whether a "visit" (a reference to how many times a page is opened) is carried out by the same person or different people. However, when a Web site forces the use of a password to gain entry, this is one way in which to keep better track of the number of different people who visit the site.

Another commonly used measure of how many people are using a Web site is called a "hit," which measures the opening of a page in addition to looking at pictures and other elements that are opened on the page. For example, consider *MSNBC*, an Internet outlet for NBC News that reported an average number of visits to its Web site before the story broke at about 300,000 a day and as many as 830,000 individual users on a single day during the first week after the story broke. *Fox News Online* revealed that the Clinton story doubled its normal daily traffic of about 1 million pages served up to computer users. The *New York Times* said that its traffic increased 20% to 30%. Approximately 13 million people visited *CNN Interactive* on the day that the president denied having the affair. This number of visits compares with the busiest day ever, close to 14 million pages viewed, which occurred when the stock market plunged. Normal daily traffic is closer to 8 million pages viewed.

Up until the story about Clinton broke, news organizations kept the two media outlets separated, both physically and culturally. Most acknowledge that the Internet provides both faster and more in-depth reporting than do television and newspapers. However, at the same time, information conveyed over the

Internet needs to be filtered much more carefully because the ability to identify the source of the information might be more difficult.

As the traditional and Internet media begin to merge in a more significant manner, there will be other manifestations. First, the interactive nature of the Internet enables it to be used to conduct instantaneous polls, further magnifying the impact of public opinion on the actions of government officials. Once the information from the Internet is viewed with more credibility, it will be translated to the more traditional arm, giving this type of information a broader audience to reach. Second, the people who use the Internet as a segment of the electorate, who are known today to be better educated and have higher incomes, will have a greater voice in the dissemination of public opinion. This, of course, will change within a matter of decades as the technology becomes so widespread that virtually every home is connected to it. Finally, the lives of public officials will become even more scrutinized than now because of the immediacy of the technology. This, of course, might be a benefit or a problem to the officials, depending on the nature of the news that is transmitted. We have entered a new era with the information highway.[29]

THE FUTURE IMPACT OF THE INTERNET

In the future, the Internet will allow people access to a style of mass communication that previously was available only to a narrow class of individuals. It will give the average individual relatively inexpensive access and the ability to spread ideas of all types to people around the world.

When the printing press was invented during the 1400s by Johann Gutenberg, it basically ended the era when religious and national leaders controlled the production of and access to books and other written materials copied by scribes. In a similar way, the Internet will end the era when only wealthy communication companies can deliver information quickly to large audiences. Interestingly, both the printing press and the Internet at first were used almost exclusively for relatively benign purposes. The printing press was used to print the bible, and the Internet was used to speed up communication among academic and government institutions.

In 1515, Pope Leo X issued the following statement: "Many masters of this new craft misuse it by the circulation of works . . . which are not only unedifying to the readers but [also] injurious to their religious and moral life. . . . The head of the church must take heed [so] that which was invented for God's glory . . . does not become a curse instead of a blessing and endanger the salvation of the faithful." The pope went on to issue a call for censorship and book burnings. Will the same happen when the Internet becomes a more integral part of political life in this country? Only time will tell. But one thing is sure: The Internet definitely will alter the way in which we know politics today.[30]

Early indications in the field are that the Internet, up to this point in time, has had more influence than was expected. Public opinion surveys conducted during the 1996 elections revealed that voters received as much information from Internet sources as from magazines. However, there still is a long way for the Internet to go before it comes close to having the same impact as does television. One point that needs to be made here is that the Internet does not afford the opportunity for "accidental" exposure, something that is far more likely over television. But for the purposes of a direct marketing tool to raise funds and to offer the highly involved voter a medium for seeking out information, the Internet is, in fact, a very powerful medium. It also may be a very effective medium to elaborate on an issue. Whereas television is far more effective at conveying information in a single direction, the Internet, as a direct marketing tool, opens up the door to an interaction between the campaign organization and the interested voter who wants to volunteer or donate money.[31]

There is evidence suggesting that the Internet as a direct marketing tool in politics is only going to grow in importance as we move into the next election cycles. In exit polls conducted by the Voter News Service with 70,000 voters nationwide, 26% of voters interviewed referred to themselves as regular users of the Internet. In another poll carried out by Wirthlin Worldwide soon after the 1996 presidential election, the marketing research firm owned by Reagan's former pollster, Richard Wirthlin, reported that 9% of the American voters, or about 8.5 million people nationwide, indicated that the information they found on the Internet influenced the ways in which they voted. Finally, in yet another poll carried out after the 1996 presidential election by the Pew Research Center, it was reported that 12% of more than 1,000 people surveyed said that they used the Internet to obtain information about the candidates running for office, and 3% of the voters in the Pew study indicated that the computer was their principal source of political information.[32]

So, who currently uses the Internet for political purposes? The answer is that it is not a random sample. These individuals tend to be under 35 years of age, well educated, politically independent, slightly cynical, and activist. Close to 70% are registered to vote. As activists, this segment offers great opportunities to campaigns looking for volunteers willing to work hard.[33] The Internet will offer campaigns the opportunity to communicate directly with supporters in a very efficient manner, especially if it is used to recruit people.

It is important to keep in mind that the demographic profile of the Internet user will change dramatically as the access problem is resolved. Prices will come down, and the connections to homes and public facilities will improve. The time will come in the future when most people are on-line. If the Internet is used in a "broadcast" mode, where information is used for viewing only, then it will closely mirror the broadcast mode of television. However, the big difference will lie with the potential to use the Internet as a direct marketing device in a two-way format. This is where the greatest potential for direct marketers lies in the future.[34]

There are, of course, two sides to the impact that the use of the Internet as a direct marketing tool will have on politics in general. On the positive side, the argument is made that Internet campaigning can level the playing field for third-party and poorly funded challengers. Furthermore, candidate Web sites can facilitate extensive discussion of issues. The Internet also offers the opportunity for candidates to spend more time getting their ideas across to the voters because of the relatively inexpensive use of this form of direct marketing. Finally, there is the opportunity for candidates to present more personal information that is difficult to convey in other media. Ultimately, the Internet offers another outlet for politicians to use to make direct contact with potential voters. Technological advances in any field, if successful, offer more choices to people.

On the negative side, one argument put forward is the concern about the frequency of negative advertising on the Internet. Still others have criticized candidate Web sites as collections of electronic "brouchureware" that is simply the equivalent of literature that used to be handed out door-to-door. In 1996, in 34 Senate races, 50 out of 68 major party candidates had homepages.[35]

One of the potential dangers of the Internet to society is the avenue that it might serve for negative campaigning. It is quite conceivable that politicians will send out scandalous information anonymously. Unfortunately, there are no ways in which to verify what one reads over the Internet, which could become another outlet for small splinter groups to vent their frustrations. Instead of transmitting over radio, as many have begun to do, they do the same over the Internet. We, as a society, will have to think about the implications of forcing people to be accountable for what they say in the public domain on political matters. Currently, there are no regulations on political speech.

This technology also has the potential to give even more power to highly energized and well-financed interest groups that participate in recruiting people to vote in the primaries. As it is now, few people vote in primaries but have a tremendous impact on the system. This could shift the power further away from the two major political parties and closer to interest groups. The financial support from a political party that used to be necessary to pay for television and print ads no longer is needed with the availability of cost-effective communication avenues such as the Internet. One firm, the American Political Network, is setting up the necessary ingredients to create an interactive democracy with a database of information on candidates into which voters can tap. This will be the beginning of an interactive democracy (or cyberdemocracy).[36]

One of the most avid users of the Internet has been interest groups. One only has to get on-line to see their formidable presence. In fact, it has been the Christian Coalition and Perot's United We Stand America that were some of the early adopters of this technology, setting up homepages and offering legislative guides and scorecards of members of Congress to interested viewers. Although there are an estimated 25 million to 40 million Americans who can potentially be reached over the Internet, a *Newsweek* poll found that only 4% of Americans had used the Web in its early stages. However, with several companies now offering access to the Web, that percentage is quickly rising.

The Internet gives hate groups the opportunity to spread their vicious messages in a very efficient manner. It takes as little as $3,000 a year for an organization to set up a Web homepage and electronic links to affiliated groups and on-line membership forms. The homepages of some of these groups are painted swastikas, skulls, and other hate symbols. Cyber-hate groups also have targeted Internet discussion groups on the Usenet network as part of their strategies for recruiting new members. There currently are more than 10,000 Usenet groups that cover an array of topics from philosophy to recipes.[37]

Individuals with agendas to share with others, referred to as "pirate" broadcasters, who since 1990 had to rely on low-watt, high-intensity stations, now have the capability to air their public opinions using the Internet, getting their message out to a far wider audience. Since 1978, the Federal Communications Commission (FCC) ruled that any AM or FM transmitter under 100 watts is illegal, arguing that such a transmitter potentially interferes with aviation, police, and emergency radio bands as well as with licensed commercial stations. However, the FCC's ban has not stopped hundreds of unlicensed stations from going on the air across the country and around the world. They refer to themselves as "micro radio" or "free radio" advocates. These so-called pirates are sharing information, and sometimes even recorded programming, over the Internet. One estimate identified from 300 to 400 such stations in operation in this country. The growing radio rebellion has been explained as a response to the domination of the airwaves by media giants as well as the absence of community-focused broadcasting. The Internet will open the door to more effective communication of this sort.[38]

One possible scenario is that a virtual Congress connected together with phones, faxes, computers, and videoconferencing would allow congresspersons to work from offices out of their own states. A virtual Congress would bring with it many serious changes in government. For example, it would make it more difficult for lobbyists to make easy face-to-face contact with a person from Congress. It would even be possible to create a panel of voters similar to the panels that companies create to rate product use and television viewership. The group members would be wired up across the nation with ratings gadgets that allowed them to express their opinions about legislation instantaneously. Using this technology, major television networks have focus groups that watch presidential State of the Union addresses or debates and rate the politicians as they listen to their speeches. In this manner, the viewers watching can get an immediate read on which messages are preferred by the focus group. It is possible for the Internet technology to bring the disenfranchised citizens and voters back into the process.[39]

CONCLUSION

Politics in the United States has turned into entertainment, where the politicians and the media personalities have become celebrities. Politicians jockey back and forth between running for office and appearing on television as "armchair quarterbacks," adding insight on the ebb and flow of a campaign. Witness the movement of Jesse Jackson, who shifts between running for the presidency and having his own news program on CNN. Similarly, Pat Buchanan, who ran for the presidency as a Republican in 1996, appeared almost nightly on *Crossfire,* one of the most popular programs on CNN. There is a symbiotic relationship between the two industries, with each one using the other to further its own interests.

A "horse race" mentality in politics has developed in the United States today, with form over substance dominating the nature of the news reporting. The media help to create the winners during the course of a campaign and then are there to clip their wings in their spiral downward. Why? Because it makes for good news, and that is what the American public is interested in seeing. The headlines in any political race center on the latest poll results. In fact, it is not uncommon for the major news stations to have focus groups monitoring a presidential debate, with instantaneous results on how well each candidate did complete with visual graphs on the television screen.

People in the United States are so time starved that information must be delivered in short, discrete sound bites if it is to be processed by the receivers. This has significant implications for the candidate who seeks to get the attention of the voters. Clearly, the medium of choice is television simply because of the potential impact it has on reinforcing and changing attitudes of the electorate. It is easier to get the attention of a television viewer than of a person listening to the radio or reading the newspaper. Political information also is more likely to be processed by the viewer if it is seen over television because images, not facts and information, are what need to be conveyed to change voter attitudes. The ability of the candidate to communicate his or her message on both a rational and an emotional plane is enhanced with television over any other medium.

One has to question the impact that the information highway is having on our democracy. On the one hand, it is healthy. It brings the alienated voters and citizens into the political process because it is more convenient for them to participate. In 1992, the voters who were disgusted with the Democratic and Republican candidates could have simply called Brown's or Perot's 800 number and joined the candidate's organization. Likewise, the voters in 1996 who sat around their homes watching Dole during one of his debates with Clinton, and who otherwise would not get involved in the political debate, had the opportunity to contact Dole's Web site (after correcting the erroneous e-mail address given out) and get more information. The information highway makes participating in the political process as easy as it is to buy products from the Home Shopping Network.

On the other hand, moving the public debate and flow of political information from the more traditional channels into telemarketing campaigns or onto the Internet turns the electoral process into a system that escapes the normal checks and balances. As the political parties continue to diminish in power, the American people will turn to the media to pick up their awesome responsibility of screening out the politicians who are fabricating the truth and conducting their affairs in an unethical manner. This will become more difficult as the Internet is used by more citizens to get their political information.

NOTES

1. Tackett, M. (1995a, May 25). Candidates go on-line to net votes. *Chicago Tribune*, sec. 1, pp. 1, 22.

2. Neikirk, W. (1996c, August 20). Crash's reminder: President never travels alone. *Chicago Tribune*, sec. 1, p. 3.

3. Newman, B. I. (1994). *The marketing of the president: Political marketing as campaign strategy.* Thousand Oaks, CA: Sage.

4. Grigsby, J. (1996, Fall). Catching up to political ads. *Public Relations Quarterly, 41,* 31-33.

5. For an excellent review of the role of the media in politics today, see Perloff, R. (1997). *Political communication: Politics, press, and public in America.* Hillsdale, NJ: Lawrence Erlbaum.

6. Terris, M., & Jaye, E. (1995, September). The art of the self-mailer: How to grab attention step-by-step. *Campaigns & Elections*, pp. 34-35.

7. Thurber, J. A., & Nelson, C. J. (Eds.). (1995). *Campaigns and elections American style.* Boulder, CO: Westview.

8. For an excellent review of the role of the Internet in politics, see Johnson, D. W. (in press). *No place for amateurs: The professionalization of modern campaigns.* London: Routledge.

9. Coates, J. (1995a, April 2). Finding poetry in the Net. *Chicago Tribune*, sec. 7, pp. 1, 4.

10. Coates, J. (1995b, April 3). Untangling the Web. *Chicago Tribune*, sec. 3, p. 1.

11. Cortese, A., & Verity, J. (1995, February 27). Cyberspace. *Business Week,* pp. 78-86.

12. Beher, R. (1997, February 3). Who's reading your e-mail? *Fortune*, pp. 57-70.

13. Peterson, R., Balasubramanian, S., & Bronnenberg, B. J. (1997). Exploring the implications of the Internet for consumer marketing. *Journal of the Academy of Marketing Science, 4,* 329-346.

14. Miller, L. (1996, October 9). Oh, what a tangled Web of studies. *USA Today,* pp. D1-D2.

15. Grumman, C. (1996, October 8). Dole error hurts Web site plug. *Chicago Tribune,* sec. 1, p. 19.

16. Associated Press. (1995b, January 6). New Internet link lets world watch Congress. *Chicago Tribune,* sec. 1, p. 11.

17. Locin, M. (1995, December 26). Cyber chant: Whole world is interacting. *Chicago Tribune,* sec. 2, pp. 1-2.

18. Democracy and technology. (1995, June 17). *The Economist,* pp. 21-23.

19. Slocum, W. (1996, April). Voter services in cyberspace. *Campaigns & Elections,* pp. 45-52.

20. Griffin, J. L. (1995, May 4). More campaigns spinning a political Web. *Chicago Tribune,* sec. 2, pp. 1, 4.

21. Noble, P. (1996, July). Net the vote. *Campaigns & Elections,* pp. 27-31.

22. Cochran, W. (1996, April). The boys on the Net. *American Journalism Review,* pp. 40-42.

23. Rubel, C. (1995, August). TV still powerful, but Web sites offer new stump for pols. *Marketing News,* pp. 5-6.

24. See Cochran (Note 22).

25. Goff, L. (1996, September 2). The Webbing of the president. *ComputerWorld,* pp. 79-80.

26. Coates, J. (1998, January 22). Internet gossip monger makes front page splash. *Chicago Tribune,* sec. 1, p. 13.

27. Stevenson, S. (1998, January 22). Invisible ink: How the story everyone's talking about stayed out of the papers. *Slate: Tangled Web.*

28. Tech report. (1998, January 23). *USA Today.*

29. Bigness, J. (1998, January 30). Clinton's crisis, Internet's boom. *Chicago Tribune,* sec. 2, p. 1.

30. Zorn, E. (1995, December 14). Internet freedom calls up worries of a bygone era. *Chicago Tribune,* sec. 2, p. 1.

31. Klotz, R. (1997). Positive spin: Senate campaigning on the Web. *Political Science & Politics, 30,* 482-486.

32. Browning, G. (1997, June/July). Updating electronic democracy. *Database,* p. 53.

33. See Noble (Note 21).

34. Guernsey, L. (1996, May 3). The electronic soapbox. *Chronicle of Higher Education,* p. A29.

35. See Klotz (Note 31).

36. See Tackett (Note 1).

37. Sheppard, N., Jr. (1995, December 12). Hate groups embrace cyberspace as weapon. *Chicago Tribune,* sec. 1, pp. 1, 23.

38. Smith, W. (1997, February 8). Defiant radio piratestuning out FCC. *Chicago Tribune,* sec. 1, pp. 1, 11.

39. Van, J. (1997, April 27). Telecommuter Congress. *Chicago Tribune,* sec. 2, pp. 1, 4.

5

Strategy

No part of the education of a politician is more indispensable than the fighting of elections.
                    —Winston Churchill, *Great Contemporaries* (1937)

According to Tom Peters, noted business guru, there are certain rules that should be followed to avoid product failure. There needs to be continuous improvement, a quality orientation, constant reengineering, empowerment to employees, and excellent customer service to boost a company's competitiveness.

But new products continue to fail on a regular basis for several reasons. First, a top executive might push a favorite idea through despite negative marketing research findings. Second, an idea might be good but the market size is overestimated. Third, the product might not be well designed. Fourth, the product might be incorrectly positioned in the market. Fifth, the advertising might not be effective.

There also might be a shortage of important new product ideas in certain areas such as ways in which to improve some products (e.g., steel, detergents). There might be social and governmental constraints on new products, which have to satisfy public criteria such as consumer safety and ecological compatibility. Government requirements slow innovation in many industries. New product development time has been speeded up significantly over the years, making it possible for competitors to get the same idea at the same time, with victory going to the swiftest. Alert companies have to compress development time by using computer and manufacturing techniques, joint partners, and the like. There is a shorter product life cycle (the duration of the life of a product in the marketplace) these days because rivals are so quick to copy ideas that the product's life cycle is shortened considerably. Sony used to enjoy a 3-year lead time on its new products before they were copied extensively by competitors. Now, Matsushita and others can copy the product within 6 months.

The formula for successful product development follows some basic rules. A successful company spends a lot of time studying the needs of target customers and getting their reactions and suggestions as the product moves through development. Second, a successful company makes the customer part of the development team. Third, it gets the support of a high company officer and advocate. Fourth, the successful company spends a lot of time announcing the new product, not leaving this step to chance. Finally, a successful new product development requires the company to establish an effective organization for managing the new product development process. Booz, Allen & Hamilton, a well-known business consulting firm, studied new product management through a mail survey of 700 consumer and industrial companies and interviews with 150 new product executives. Some key findings were that management had success with 65% of its product launches and that companies developed one successful product for every seven they researched.[1]

Success in a presidential campaign is subject to a similar set of rules, but in a much more condensed time period. In fact, if we can look back at some of the most recent presidential campaigns, the successes and failures of well-known political leaders can be explained by taking a critical look at the marketing strategies each one followed. Let us take a closer look at some winning and losing political campaign strategies through the years.

REAGAN IN 1980: A SUCCESS /
CARTER IN 1980: A FAILURE

In 1980, Ronald Reagan's timing could not have been better. Jimmy Carter had just finished going through a tumultuous period that left his image damaged and looking weak because of a frail economy and the hostage crisis in Iran. The country was eager for a president who would bring back a more regal feeling in the White House. To further complicate Carter's situation, he was an incumbent who was challenged from within his own party by Ted Kennedy.

Richard Wirthlin, Reagan's pollster, believed that three pivotal tactical decisions in the campaign turned it around for Reagan: running a 6-week series of advertisements on Reagan's record as California governor, having Reagan avoid personal criticism of Carter, and having Reagan debate Carter. Wirthlin also believed that Carter's personal attacks on Reagan damaged Carter's own image more than they hurt Reagan's. Carter wound up manufacturing an image of himself as mean-spirited.

One of Carter's big failures was letting the challenger look more "presidential" than the president himself. This happened to Carter toward the end of the campaign. As Election Day came closer and closer, it was obvious that the role Reagan was preparing for started to look as if he were actually playing it for many years. An actor is supposed to be able to "become" the person he or she is playing. Reagan's many years of acting definitely were an asset. At the same time, Carter's frustration with the Iranian hostage crisis clearly was wearing on him, dragging him down emotionally.

Reagan effectively made Carter's record the issue. Carter's problem was that he never resolved what it was he wanted to say about his administration; he did not have a vision for the next 4 years.

Most of the decisions in the Carter campaign were made through a consensus by five people: Hamilton Jordan, Carter's chief of staff; Robert Strauss, the campaign chairman; Jody Powell, the press secretary; Patrick Caddell, the pollster; and Gerald Rafshoon, the publications media specialist. It is clear from Carter's failure that a campaign must be spearheaded by a single individual, not by a five-headed strategist.

Of course, one cannot dismiss the fact that public dissatisfaction with the economy probably hurt Carter more than any other single issue. The pocketbook issue in politics is the lens that all citizens look through to evaluate a presidential candidate. If the economy is not strong and people are hurting financially, then the incumbent is seen in a much more negative light than the challenger.[2]

REAGAN IN 1984: A SUCCESS / MONDALE IN 1984: A FAILURE

Reagan's reelection campaign in 1984 was successful for a number of reasons. One of the main factors behind his success was the coordinating mechanism between the White House and the campaign structure, which was set up early. That group consisted of Jim Baker, Mike Deaver, Dick Darman, and Margaret Tutwiler, all of whom got along very well. Later called the campaign strategy group, the four met an average of 4 hours a week throughout the campaign. Ed Rollins was the bridge between them and the campaign structure. Rollins and Lee Atwater moved out of the White House to run the campaign operation. Jim Baker was the conduit between the outside organization and the White House.

The Reagan people used the primaries to build up a grassroots organization and extensive voter list, targeting specific demographic groups in every state. Political operatives who were with Reagan from 1976 and 1980 were weeded out and replaced with others such as Illinois Governor Jim Thompson and Texas Senator John Tower to run state operations. Baker, the chief of staff, was the linchpin that connected the president to any activity during the campaign. Every effort was made to ensure that the economy was robust and that America was at peace during the time of the general election. Remember, a world at peace and a strong economy make it very easy for a sitting president to manufacture a winning image.

A crucial decision, according to Rollins, was to avoid at all costs the involvement of people in the White House who thought that they were engaged in a political campaign. Rollins made sure that those duties were left to the campaign organization.

Also of tremendous help were observations by Atwater about issues that affected prior incumbent presidents such as to avoid a bad relationship between the White House and the campaign organization, that the campaign organization must become a "mini-White House" but at the same time be limited in its responsibilities, that campaign organization activities must include voter registration and "get out the vote," to avoid duplicating activities in the White House, and to avoid leaking back and forth between the White House and the organization as to "who's in and who's out" of the campaign.

Something else that the Reagan people did was keep tight controls on expenditures during the campaign. To avoid people in the field feeling left out of the information loop in Washington, D.C., and at the same time feeling empowered, meetings were held in the field with campaign workers during the spring and summer of 1984. While the general election started in April 1984 with a media program set up to offset the expected attacks of Walter Mondale, the Reagan campaign waited to talk about the economy until it strengthened.

At the same time, Mondale's campaign failed because of the inability of the candidate to communicate with his audience over television. Mondale's commercials were confusing and difficult to follow. Unlike Reagan's simple and easy-to-follow themes of patriotism, Mondale's themes seemed to center on "tax and spend" issues. Perhaps Mondale's biggest failure was in his inability to convey an image of the person he was in real life. In person, Mondale was said to be easygoing and fun to be around. However, on television, he came across as stiff and uptight. Unfortunately for Mondale, the television age had already hit politics, and his inability to use it to his advantage killed his image and ultimately his campaign.[3]

BUSH IN 1988: A SUCCESS / DUKAKIS IN 1988: A FAILURE

In 1988, George Bush made Michael Dukakis "the issue" of the campaign. The general election campaign started in May 1988. Atwater was put in charge of the opposition research department. Roger Ailes was given control over delivery of Bush's "message," which included speeches, interviews, and advertising. Bush's themes were simple and few ("Read my lips," and "A kinder, gentler nation"), allowing him to manufacture an image that was consistent with the desire on the part of the electorate not to have its taxes raised. Ailes demanded—

and received—direct access to Bush anytime and had the authority to sit in on any meetings. In a campaign, there can be only one media guru. Bush had Ailes. Dukakis, on the other hand, never had just one guru, and this hurt him badly. Bush empowered his people and let his handlers do their jobs; Dukakis did not.

Bush's organization chart had clearly defined responsibilities. There would be control over the state parties, enlisting them to go only as far as the organization wanted them to go. The "Willie Horton" issue was taken too far by the state parties, ostensibly pushed by "independent committees," but at the same time was terribly effective in shaping Dukakis's image.

Ultimately, the purpose of the campaign organization should be defined early on, something that Bush did effectively. Bush's staff met every day from May 1988 onward to decide on the "message of the day," the "message of the week," and where the campaign was headed. Bush's position in the marketplace was very consistent throughout the campaign because the candidate himself remained focused, with a comprehensive game plan that was implemented with discipline.

At the top, only Atwater and Ailes met every day. One of the great lessons to learn from this campaign is that the person who is in constant touch with the campaign organization must be with the candidate every day, all the time to ensure that the candidate follows through with the strategy. This is a strategy that Bush's organization followed and Dukakis's did not.

The campaign organization cannot be run by only one person. There must be four or five people who are given all the turf they can handle. This is critical to ensure that the candidate is free to stay on top of the message he is sending. He is then in a better position to reinforce the image created in the ads. Bush also avoided bringing in people too late to the campaign who did not have his confidence.

The opposition research department headed by Atwater generated 125,000 quotes from 436 different sources. The Bush people identified five or six issues by mid-May, which were put on 3×5 cards and carried around by all the top staffers. A second card generated from the research centered on five or six issues about the challenger. The Bush people assumed that the American people voted in cycles and that if Reagan Democrats did not see a difference between Bush and Dukakis, then they would switch back to Dukakis, so they worked hard to define those differences. Bush exploited and used the power of the Reagan presidency by having Reagan stump for him and postpone unpopular decisions until after the campaign was over. Bush did make some mistakes in this campaign. His handlers had him in interview situations for which he was either too tired or ill prepared.

By contrast, Dukakis never understood the importance of firing right back when attacked by one's opponent with a negative commercial. From the very beginning, Dukakis decided to turn his cheek to the attacks that Bush hit him with over and over again. In the process, Dukakis was labeled as weak and ineffective. In effect, Dukakis lost control over the manufacturing of his own image. At the same time, Bush reengineered his own image and, in the process, eliminated the "wimp" label he had been fighting for a long time. As a result, Bush looked to be the stronger leader of the two candidates.[4]

BUSH IN 1992: A FAILURE /
CLINTON IN 1992: A SUCCESS

In 1992, the Republican Convention was planned largely by party officials outside the control of the campaign. As a result, millions of voters were alienated from the right-wing oratory in what should have been a major sales pitch for Bush. The lessons learned were to maintain tight control over the convention from within the campaign organization and to make sure that every speech is read before it gets the "green light" (Pat Buchanan's speech was not and went on to criticize policies that Bush was advocating). The Bush campaign was operating without help from the White House. The Bush White House was so disorganized that political directions changed daily, and it took 7 months to hire a speechwriter for the president.

With 11 weeks until Election Day, Bush still had $40 million to spend on commercials, a week-long convention, and debates on the horizon. In addition, he had just persuaded Jim Baker to return to impose order on the chaos. But Baker brought neither purpose nor focus to the campaign. Basically, the Bush campaign organization had no strategy. One of the biggest "mechanical break-downs" in the campaign organization was not demanding censorship rights over any convention speech. While party loyalists played at the Astrodome in Houston, Texas, Bush's top campaign advisers closeted themselves at the suburban Doubletree Hotel—a serious mistake.

The relationship between the campaign organization and the advertising people was horrible. Bob Teeter lured Madison Avenue's top talent to a new advertising agency dubbed "The November Company," whose sole task was to create Bush's television commercials. But an entire summer was wasted on debate over whether the advertising executives or the campaign should be in charge of what to say. The ad executives complained that the campaign people did not know what they wanted to say, and the campaign people never liked anything the ad executives gave them. This resulted in focus groups deciding what would run—a huge mistake. Focus groups, although an effective market-ing tool at generating ideas for issues, images, and the like, are not a random representation of the population at large and always should be followed up with a full-blown marketing research study on a random selection of the electorate.

Bush's strategy during the final 10 weeks of the campaign included a 3-week introduction to the president's second-term economic agenda, a few weeks to compare that agenda favorably to Clinton's "higher priced" economic proposals, and a concluding barrage of commercials emphasizing Bush's experience and stature and maligning Clinton's image by comparison.

The November Company found negative commercials distasteful and refused to run them, even in response to negative attacks by Clinton. Baker had to hire a B-advertising (i.e., second-rate) team to put together negative ads, a team headed by Mitch Daniels, an Indiana political adviser brought into the campaign in August. Because Daniels had to go to Japan for other business, the inventory of commercials was slim in September, so Baker brought in Sig Rogich, one of the brains behind the Reagan and Bush advertising campaigns in 1984 and 1988. Rogich produced six commercials and became the architect of the campaign's increasingly negative tone on television. The lesson to be learned from this was that a totally disorganized campaign organization that got started too late on the wrong foot makes for a bad competitor in a presidential race.

From a strategic point of view, Clinton's success as a candidate can be attributed to the flexibility he maintained throughout the campaign, beginning with a message of change that resonated well in the ears of voters throughout the primary season. However, once he entered the convention stage, Clinton repositioned his theme of change around the economy. Bush, on the other hand, was trying to reposition his image from the time he won the war in Iraq. He seemed to be fixated on the image of himself as the leader of the Western world and the one candidate who could be relied on in the case of a crisis.

During the campaign, Clinton was focused on two things: the economy and change. A sign hung in the "war room" that read "It's the Economy, Stupid," a message that the whole campaign organization never forgot. This message worked to Clinton's advantage, as he was able to use it as the glue holding together all dimensions of his marketing strategy including speeches, commercials, support by other politicians, and the like.[5]

THE REPUBLICAN REVOLUTION OF 1994: A SUCCESS

The 1994 election found the country yearning for more change, similar to the "mantra" that Americans had voiced in the 1992 election. There was a desire for less government, and both parties campaigned on this platform. There was a wholesale slaughter of Democratic congresspersons in the 1994 midterm election. Waiting patiently as a back-bencher in Congress for more than 15 years, Newt Gingrich rose to the top in 1994. Relying on pollster Frank Luntz to carry out marketing research that identified the wording of the "Contract With America," Gingrich and his army of Republicans dominated the airwaves and responded to voters' needs with a very effective marketing strategy. With a carefully orchestrated campaign chock full of hype and media sensationalism, the Republican Party took control of the House of Representatives for the first time in 40 years.

In one of the latest technological advances in the 1994 campaign, Republicans put a little movie magic called "morfing" into their marketing efforts. The technique was mastered in the movie *The Terminator.* In a 5- to 10-second period, actor Arnold Schwarzenegger changes from man to machine, making it seem as if Schwarzenegger and The Terminator are the same person. Republican candidates capitalized on Clinton's ebb in the polls and morfed their Democratic opponents into Clinton. The impact of this imagery was felt by the Democrats, who went down in defeat in the Republican revolution of 1994.

In September 1994, soon after Gingrich announced the Contract With America, the Republican National Committee lined up nearly 300 talk radio interviews through the Virginia Contract Information Center. The network has 500 radio talk shows on its fax network, and hosts of these shows were sent pro-contract press clippings and talking points for the contract. Many of the radio show hosts read the clippings verbatim. The success of the contract was due in large part to this marketing effort.

Many people who voted for the Contract With America did so without fully understanding the implications of some of its amendments. People did not care about specifics when they voted to throw the Democrats out of Congress. Voters, the middle class in particular, just wanted more and more change. And the polls revealed an electorate totally distrusting of Clinton and, more important, fed up with his inability to keep his promises, particularly the one calling for a middle class tax cut. These same people were willing to buy the contract that promised more and better change.

The Republicans' victory in 1994 was capitalized on by using the Contract With America as a "postelection" marketing tool. In response to the successful marketing of the contract after the election, the president introduced his Middle Class Bill of Rights, a "new and improved" version of the Republicans' contract. Each of these efforts reflected a move toward the political center, where the most votes could be attracted.

Just as consumers sometimes do not read labels on products, neither do citizens always listen carefully to what politicians say. On his first day as speaker of the House, Gingrich talked about Franklin D. Roosevelt with high praise for the way in which he made government work in his first 100 days. Gingrich failed to mention, of course, that he was setting out to dismantle the very programs that were put into place during Roosevelt's time. Voters do, however, pay close attention to what politicians actually do. Promises might work to get a politician elected, but delivering is the essential ingredient for continued success in office. This is evident from the dramatic rise in the polls for the Republicans 100 days after they delivered on most elements in the contract.

The midterm election of 1994 was labeled by Ralph Nader as a "turning point in the dissolution of the two-party system," with both parties moving closer to the middle. Nader pointed out that it is increasingly difficult to distinguish between Democrats and Republicans and that the two parties, in fact, represent the same party with different names. He even jokingly referred to them as the "Demopublicans" or "Republocrats."

CLINTON IN 1996: A SUCCESS /
DOLE IN 1996: A FAILURE

Clinton successfully repositioned himself for the 1996 presidential election by drawing a comparison between himself, the leader of the Democratic Party, and Gingrich, the unannointed leader of the Republican Party. The contrast in images turned out to be startling to the American people. In fact, the Republicans' successful marketing of the Contract With America turned into a contract on the very life of the Republican Party 2 years after many claimed its victory to be a revolution. If it was a revolution, then it was a very short-lived one.

Perhaps the single most significant event that took place between the 1994 and 1996 elections was the decision on the part of the Clinton administration to sign the budget bill advanced by the Republicans. In one swift move, this repositioned the Democratic Party and the president to the center of the political spectrum. In effect, Clinton adopted a more conservative campaign platform, one that, on some issues, was advocated by the Republican Party. In fact, the public relations battle that was waged by both the Republicans (led by Gingrich, Dole, and Dick Armey) and Democrats (led by Clinton, Gore, and Richard Gephardt) clearly was won by the Democrats when the Republicans threatened to shut down the government. That did not play very well with the American people. In fact, from October 1995 right through to the election in November 1996, Clinton's approval ratings consistently increased to a clear victory at the polls.

As a result of the budget battle and carefully orchestrated media events, such as the televised debate between Clinton and Gingrich, Gingrich eventually self-destructed. Leaks from the budget battle that associated Gingrich with supporting the elimination of lunches for schoolchildren and other welfare-related issues painted an image of Gingrich as a mean-spirited politician. The image that was created with his successful marketing of the Contract With America was literally destroyed over a period of 1 year. Part of the problem was Gingrich's conviction that there was a revolution going on, and he was the leader by default ever since Clinton's ratings had plummeted in the polls around the time of the November 1994 election. Along with the destruction of Gingrich came that of the Republican Party and Dole, neither of which could shake their connections to Gingrich. If one were to package the Republican Party leading up the 1996 election, the label would have a big picture of Gingrich on the front of it.

At the same time, Clinton repositioned himself from a Washington insider to a Washington outsider. This was due, in part, to the "triangulation" strategy recommended to him by Dick Morris. With this strategy, Clinton positioned himself at the apex of a triangle, juxtaposed against the two political parties. In other words, Clinton successfully repositioned himself as a leader of the free world—not as either a Democrat or a Republican—and, at the same time, adopted issues and policies of both parties so as not to be labeled as either conservative or liberal. During this same period, the image that was cast of the president changed dramatically, from being shown in his jogging shorts eating at McDonald's to sitting in the Rose Garden at the White House, looking statesmanlike and signing documents with leaders from around the world.

Another factor that led to Clinton's successful strategy in 1996 was changing the attitude of the media toward him. In effect, Clinton quickly became the kinder and gentler president, treating the media with silk gloves instead of with brass knuckles. Clinton learned the hard way that the media are the opinion leaders (or retailers) in his business, those who have the power to either tarnish or polish the president's image.

The Republicans deserve as much blame for their failures during the 1996 campaign as Clinton deserves credit for his successes. The primary battle was a tough one, with successful bids by a number of marginal candidates. Steve Forbes, who used a simple flat tax as the central focus of his marketing campaign and close to $35 million of his own money, literally put himself onto the national political map. One of his early mistakes was not winning over the support of the Christian Coalition due to some ill-advised statements made during the Iowa caucus. An important part of designing the product in politics is gaining the support from critical interest groups.

Buchanan was another outside candidate who made a serious bid for the Republican nomination. It was not until Buchanan's upset win in the New Hampshire primary that the Republican Party realized it had to act fast to ensure that Buchanan did not become the nominee. With every victory, Buchanan became more and more confident, soon donning a black hat in one of the western primaries. This did not help his image, which was built on a populist appeal and his ability to reach out to those who were hurting economically. Soon afterward, Dole was put into the fast lane by the leaders of the Republican Party and became the nominee. Although the political parties see their power waning with every new campaign, at the presidential level, they can still exert an awful lot of influence if they choose to do so.

Dole was potentially a strong candidate, but the Republicans still lost. The mistakes by Dole were numerous, from leaving the Senate to campaign full-time to advocating a 15% tax cut that, in the depths of his heart, he himself clearly did not believe was realistic. His main message, the 15% tax cut, was one that he had voted against earlier in his career. Dole tried unsuccessfully to position himself as the outsider by leaving the Senate, wearing leisure suits, and trying to play down his insider role. Unfortunately, images of him built up over a 30-year career as a professional politician were not easily forgotten by the American people. In the end, his campaign seemed disingenuous and one that was marketing a false image of the man.

If there is one lesson to learn from Dole's mistakes in this campaign, it is that a marketing strategy must match the product. Dole was the ultimate insider to the American people, an image that could have been played on more successfully if his handlers had carried out their marketing research differently. As an insider, Dole could have been positioned as the one politician who, with his understanding of the inner workings of Congress, would be able to put an end to future gridlock in Washington.

Even though the Republicans had an ineffectual product that was mispositioned to the American people, they conducted their convention in a very effective manner. Elizabeth Dole carried off a commanding performance during her speech, ensuring her presence as a voice in her party for years to come. The Christian Coalition was effectively silenced at the convention, a definite public relations plus with the American people but a thorn in the side of the party, one that would be felt later when it came time for the coalition to come out in strong support of the party's nominee.

The marketing strategies of the two major candidates differed significantly. Clinton pushed to restore the "American Dream" for the children of America. He pushed education as a way up the ladder for middle class citizens. His message was positive and constructive. Clinton focused on voters' concerns, not his own concerns. Clinton did not have an intraparty fight (especially not from Jesse Jackson) during the primaries, unlike the intraparty fights the Democratic Party had to cope with in previous recent elections. This helped Clinton to consolidate his base. Unfortunately for Dole, the grueling primary that pushed him to the right to win over the ultraconservative Christian Coalition support hurt his moderate image badly during the general election. A lesson to be learned here is that images can be remanufactured, but it takes time.

Dole attempted to appeal to the American people with a message of fear and unrealistic hope that a 15% tax cut would make all their problems go away. Dole's message was simply not believable. Dole thought that Jack Kemp would add a sustainable boost to his candidacy as his running mate. Unfortunately, the boost was only temporary. Furthermore, Dole constantly was changing campaign staff, leaving his organization disjointed and disillusioned.

THE 1998 ELECTION: THE FALL OF GINGRICH
AND THE RISE OF VENTURA

Although Clinton was not an announced candidate for office in the 1998 election, he clearly was running against Gingrich. Most people were caught off-guard by Gingrich's decision to resign from his post as majority leader of the House of Representatives and his position in Congress. Who would have imagined that only 3 months after the president acknowledged an inappropriate relationship with Monica Lewinsky, Gingrich would resign? The only explanation one can provide is the ability of the president to continue to manufacture an image in the eyes of the public that keeps his approval ratings up in the polls.

Still, Republican Party leaders have to wonder how it was possible that they could have lost five seats in the House and a couple of governorships that they thought were in their camp. If one couples the staunch anti-Clinton message that Gingrich sent with his $10 million advertising blitz questioning the integrity of the president with the success of the Bush brothers in their bids to win the governorships of Texas (George) and Florida (Jeb), then it appears that a new strategy emerged for the Republicans: Be pragmatic and much less ideological to reach out to the more moderate voters and perhaps even attract a few Democrats along the way.

Gingrich tried to reengineer his manufactured image around the president's sexual escapades and alleged wrongdoing. He went so far as to predict that the president would be made to pay for his sins, resulting in the Republicans picking up from 6 to 30 seats in Congress. After the election was over, Gingrich admitted that he misjudged the electorate. Gingrich further miscalculated when negotiating with the president on the budget deal and was convinced that he could get what he wanted despite the president's strong showing in the polls. The image manufactured by the president for the Democrats in both the budget deal and the election was of a president and a party that were trying to attend to their business while Gingrich and the Republicans were trying to bring the president down. Unfortunately for Gingrich, he not only did not reengineer his image, he ultimately destroyed it.

By talking issues, the same way in which he did when Morris advised the president 2 years before his reelection in 1996 to begin announcing one new policy each week, the president refabricated his image by showing a side of it to the American people that they seemed to understand. Images, like a product, can be viewed from many different sides, depending on how one holds it and from what angle one looks at it. Clinton has mastered the art of letting the American people see the side of his image that he wants them to see. After hearing the president beat down by experts on cable television stations for 3 consecutive months since his summer admission, the public became fed up with the constant onslaught, and the situation reached a point where Americans said that enough is enough. The president never forgot the lesson he learned in his 1992 election victory, that is, the importance of reading the polls and taking a market orientation to policy initiatives. Based on testimony reported by independent counsel Ken Starr, we now know that the president continued to poll throughout the summer and fall, and he read the tea leaves in the polls that told him that the American people wanted him to continue doing his job. The Republicans had access to the same polls but chose not to believe them. This was a mistake, and they paid for it dearly in the election. Perhaps the biggest mistake that the Republicans made strategically was to let the $10 million advertising campaign questioning the president's integrity run days before the election.

At the same time, the Democrats employed one of the best strategic initiatives they could have employed, that is, relying on Hillary Rodham Clinton to rally the crowds and to help restore the president's broken image in the minds of many. In one of the more interesting strategic ploys by the Democrats, they had the first lady record close to 100 phone scripts and radio spots and had the phone messages left automatically on thousands of opinion leaders' machines all over the country. In addition, she went across the country and spoke at close to 50 fund-raisers and 34 rallies, bringing in millions of dollars to help pay for the advertising campaigns of selected Democratic candidates. The sight of Hillary Rodham Clinton speaking on behalf of her husband in light of the Lewinsky allegations made for great television, and it brought in more free television coverage than many candidates received. This might be the result of soaring approval ratings, rising up to 70%. Many people like her, and the Democrats took great advantage of that.[6]

Strategically, the Republicans had to deal with another political lightning rod, that is, Starr. The Starr Report that detailed the intimate details of the president's sexual encounters with Lewinsky proved to be too sensational for most people. Many wondered how closely tied Starr was to some of the right-wing organizations trying to topple the president. The Republican Party ultimately died along with Gingrich in 1998. Gingrich simply refused to read the polls and go along with public opinion. Perhaps it was that very nature that put him into the spotlight many years ago as a back-bencher in Congress when he successfully toppled the Democratic leadership in Congress.

A good marketer must remain flexible, always ready to reposition his or her ideas and policies and ever so vigilant of the polls. Gingrich's ultimate downfall was that he was not a good marketer, something proven by his dramatically low approval ratings in the polls. When he tried unsuccessfully to continue to lead the Republican Party, he failed to understand one of the most important principles in marketing: A defective product with a soiled image cannot be sold to people even if it is wrapped up in a new package and promoted with a million-dollar advertising campaign.

The level of money spent on elections continued to escalate at an unbeliev-able rate in 1998. According to Federal Election Commission records, candi-dates raised $575 million and spent $480 million between January 1, 1997, and October 14, 1998. As was the case in previous elections, the candidates who spent the most money won, with few exceptions. One of those exceptions in 1998 took place in Wisconsin, where Senator Russ Feingold, who refused to accept "soft money" contributions, won without the help of special interests. That, of course, is not to say that the interest groups still did not have an influence on the outcome.

Although the elections in 1998 witnessed continued reliance on television to promote political ideas and images, the Internet took on some new dimen-sions, with technology making it much easier for candidates to manufacture their images in a more cost-effective and sophisticated manner. Some candi-dates had operatives videotaping campaign appearances that were simultane-ously downloaded onto candidates' Web sites for those who were interested in following these appearances from the comfort of their own homes.

Another surprise in 1998 was the election of Jesse Ventura, a former wrestler, who won the governorship of Minnesota. Interestingly, he was the first Reform Party candidate (started by Ross Perot) to win a statewide office. Perhaps the election of Ventura against two highly respected politicians, Democrat Hubert Humphrey III (son of the late vice president and state attorney general) and Republican Norm Coleman (mayor of St. Paul) is the sign of an electorate that is fed up with the system. Ventura's political career began as the mayor of Brooklyn Park, a Minneapolis suburb.

Ventura campaigned on a Harley-Davidson motorcycle and clearly parlayed this same strategy in his successful bid for governor, manufacturing an image that is novel, unique, and anti-establishment and that plays well with the young people. During his campaign for governor, he smoked cigars and was proud of it. One cannot minimize the support of the Reform Party in Minnesota, where Perot won 24% of the vote during the 1992 presidential election. Furthermore, Ventura's pledge not to meddle in people's private affairs, not to increase taxes, and to return all future state budge surpluses to taxpayers, apparently struck a responsive chord with voters. In the words of one Democratic state repre-sentative, Myron Orfield, "Jesse isn't just a former wrestler. He's a cultural phenomenon. He's connected to the modern vernacular of things here. He's with it." In a word, he manufactured an image that sold very well in the marketplace.[7]

CONCLUSION

There are several key strategic lessons to learn from the recent elections that shed important light on the use and misuse of marketing strategies. Strategic thinking should be seen as an opportunity to transform an organization and change the rules of an industry to its advantage. There is no room for incremental change. Do not try to position products and businesses within an industry. Create tomorrow's industry. This is something that the Republicans and Gingrich did well in 1994 and that the Democrats and Clinton did well in 1992.

Just as companies need to partner with each other to be effective, so too do politicians. A candidate must get all partners to share his or her vision of the future. The focus should be on what can be, not what is. One never must lose sight of one's customer. Clinton has been very effective at empowering the American people and getting them to buy into his vision for the country.

Extensive consumer research must be collected on a regular basis. Sears did, and the company found out that whereas there were high levels of brand loyalty to Sears hardware lines, the do-it-yourself market, if targeted to home owners with simple jobs, also could exist without competing head-on with The Home Depot and other home improvement companies. It is a well-known fact that the Clinton campaign teams of 1992 and 1996 collected data on a regular basis to frame their political communications to the American people and were very successful because of it.

The Rubber Maid company is known for its constant innovation, coming out with unique new and interesting kitchen and household appliances that make everyday life easier for consumers. Similarly, the automobile manufacturers must come up with new models every year to satisfy consumers' desire for change. In the same way, political candidates must be constantly thinking about how they can make the government work in more efficient ways to ensure that the electorate views them as agents of change for the people as opposed to self-centered opportunists who are in politics to get rich.

Unfortunately for politicians today, we have entered a period in this country where there is an information overload in politics. Candidates are bent on running negative campaigns, and the media are pressured to provide news that entertains and keeps people's attention, resulting in information that has a sensational slant. This makes the marketing job of imagery management that much more difficult for politicians. A presidential campaign is all about making promises and shaping people's expectations. Control of information centers on having an organized staff, empowered to carry out the strategic initiatives that will be consistent with the image that is manufactured for the candidate.

Most critical to the marketing success of a political candidate is that he or she has a vision that is not subject to the vacillations of the public's reactions to the candidate's ideas or to his or her standings in the polls—a tall order indeed. The need for flexibility in a rapidly changing political environment calls for a constant monitoring of information and a chain of command that can implement strategic decisions quickly and immediately. New product development in politics is not housed in a research and development department; rather, it is housed in a simulated war room surrounded by computers, facsimile machines, and television monitors where flexibility hinges on the ability of a political organization to remanufacture a candidate's image.

NOTES

1. Booz, Allen, & Hamilton. (1982). *New products management for the 1980's.* New York: Author.

2. Institute of Politics. (1981). *Campaign for president: The managers look at '80.* Cambridge, MA: Harvard University, John F. Kennedy School of Government, Institute of Politics.

3. Institute of Politics. (1985). *Campaign for president: The managers look at '84.* Cambridge, MA: Harvard University, John F. Kennedy School of Government, Institute of Politics.

4. Institute of Politics. (1989). *Campaign for president: The managers look at '88.* Cambridge, MA: Harvard University, John F. Kennedy School of Government, Institute of Politics.

5. Goldman, P., DeFrank, T. M., Miller, M., Murr A., & Mathews, T. (1994). *Quest for the presidency 1992.* College Station: Texas A & M Press.

6. Cloud, J. (1998, November 16). Give'em hell Hillary. *Time,* p. 52.

7. Gray, P. (1998, November 16). Body slam. *Time,* p. 57.

The Art of Crafting an Image

All reality is merely text, subject to infinite interpretation and linguistic manipulation—but never to definitive judgment.
—Jacques Derrida (French theorist)

As early as Franklin D. Roosevelt's campaign, modern marketing technology has been used to create images and sell ideas in a presidential election. The main thrust of Roosevelt's efforts was on creating an image of a physically strong leader. During Roosevelt's presidential campaign, imagery management convinced voters that he could walk when in fact he was crippled. Using a technique that took him many years to master, he would lean on the side of the muscular arm of his son and use a cane in the other hand to give the illusion that he was walking when in fact he really was not.

At the time, Americans knew that Roosevelt had contracted polio, but many did not know that he was crippled from it. In close to 50,000 pictures of Roosevelt at his summer home in New York, only 2 have him sitting in a wheelchair. To convince the American people that he was not crippled, Roosevelt had the braces on his legs painted black, and always wore black pants that went down to his shoes so that the braces were hidden.

It was not until Roosevelt's final speech to Congress after the Yalta Conference, the first time that he gave a speech to Congress while he was sitting down, that he admitted to wearing 10 pounds of steel to keep him supported while he was standing. Elaborate schemes were devised for every public appearance he would make, with the Secret Service building ramps to enable him to drive up in his car to the podium. Careful attention to detail included decisions such as the placement of his chair and, most important, how he would ascend to and descend from the podium. This certainly never would have worked today in the television era in which we live, but it does demonstrate that polishing political images is not new.

Roosevelt also was a master of his personal image. He had a terrible relationship with his wife, and it was believed that he was in love with his personal secretary. After Eleanor Roosevelt found love letters in her husband's suitcase when he returned from a trip, the president and the first lady never were intimate again. But Roosevelt did have a terrific relationship with the press, and several secrets, including the estranged relationship with his wife and his crippled condition, were kept from the American people.

Despite their estrangement, Franklin and Eleanor Roosevelt forged a political alliance that kept the first lady traveling all over the country to push the president's New Deal programs. In her travels, Eleanor Roosevelt served as the eyes and ears of the president, continually monitoring public opinion and perceptions of his programs. Today, her efforts have been replaced by sophisticated polling techniques that allow a president to carry out that same monitoring function.

THE PERCEPTION OF IMAGES

One of the most important marketing tools a politician can use to drive public opinion is his or her image. Recall how John F. Kennedy used to put one hand in his suitcoat pocket or run a hand through his hair. During the 1988 presidential campaign, some accused Gary Hart of copying these gestures to help create an image of himself as the new Kennedy. In this television era of 30-second sound bites, people form attitudes about politicians in a short period of time, leaving the delivery and overall impressions left with the viewers often more important than the messages.

Ronald Reagan was a master at building an image for himself, from the photo opportunities that always had him standing in front of patriotic symbols such as the American flag to the gestures and words he used to embrace the hearts and minds of the American people.

Images are subject to the ebb and flow of a politician's ability to deal with various issues and scandals that arise. Bill Clinton's aides have dealt successfully with several potential scandals during the course of his presidency, the most sensational of which were the allegations that he had a sexual relationship with Monica Lewinsky. In fact, people have marveled at Clinton's ability to keep his approval ratings so high in the face of these allegations. By carefully crafting an image of himself as a leader in charge and almost above the rumor mongering of the media about his sex life, Clinton has been able to shape public opinion in his favor. Successful image manufacturing calls for constant monitoring of public opinion and effectively shaping the public debate.

After getting into office, every president is challenged during his tenure—whether personally, domestically, or internationally—and must rely on the ability of his consultants to keep his image as a strong leader intact with the American people. Every modern-day president, from Kennedy through Clinton, had visible episodes in the media where his image as a leader was challenged. Kennedy had the Cuban missile crisis, Lyndon Johnson had Vietnam, Richard Nixon had the Watergate scandal, Jimmy Carter had the Iranian hostage crisis, Reagan had a recession, George Bush had Iraq, and Clinton had Whitewater.

THE EMOTIONAL CONNECTION
IN POLITICS

Emotions such as fear and hope pervade modern life. Security products firms have capitalized on the use of fear for many years. Companies play on our fears with advertisements that tap into our emotional makeup. For example, a magazine ad for American Express features a black tornado with the headline "It's heading for your itinerary," suggesting to viewers that American Express has a service that can help them avert disaster.

Another example of this type of advertising can be found in a newspaper insert by S. C. Johnson Wax picturing coupons for Windex that could be used to "Clean up crime in your community." The appeal here urges consumers to work together with their neighbors to talk about ways in which to reduce the level of crime. A television spot for the Buick LeSabre features a father driving past slower moving traffic and avoiding oncoming cars as his wife and daughter are fast asleep in the car. The message flashed onto the screen says, "The message comes through, I'm responsible for my family."

The use of fear is perhaps best remembered with actor Karl Malden warning, "Don't leave home without your American Express card" and with Texaco telling car owners to "Trust your car to the man who wears the star." It should not be surprising to know that a *USA Today*/CNN/Gallup Poll listed crime and violence as the nation's most critical problems. Americans are put into a constant state of fear and then brought out of it with a message of hope. Why? Because emotion is what sells products and politicians. It also makes the use of imagery a very potent tool to ease people's fears when they view a politician standing tall and in control of a situation.[1]

Politics comes down to our gut reactions about politicians and their ideas. The emotions that we feel when we watch leaders are an integral part of how we judge politicians. Roger D. Masters has studied people's emotional reactions to politicians and believes that facial displays of fear and other emotions are a trait that humans share with other primates.

For example, Masters points to the picture of Dukakis sitting in the army tank during the 1988 presidential campaign and how that ultimately worked to kill the image of Dukakis as a serious leader. The biggest turnoff to people is when they perceive a leader's fear. According to Master's research, fear is communicated to people when the political leader looks down, hesitates, or begins to make fast and jerky motions. Perhaps the worst thing a person can do in a situation where he or she feels fear is to freeze, which is what many thought Dan Quayle did in his debate with Lloyd Bentsen in 1988. Similarly, a big grin also can be read as a sign of tension. People look to their leaders to project a sense of smoothness in the way in which they deal with others and to adapt to different and unique situations. There should not be any threatening behavior. The fact is that appearances do matter to people. Reagan's and Clinton's success as political leaders is intimately tied to their ability to put people at ease with their presence, whether appearing on television in a debate or news conference, being seen with other world leaders signing documents, or even just greeting people and shaking hands. Sometimes, all it takes is a nod of the head, a look in the eye, or a stare for just the appropriate amount of time to send the correct emotional signal to someone watching a person. A smile for a politician goes a long way because it suggests a certain ease about the individual and can even disarm the politicians' worst critics.

Similar to other primates, humans tend to spend most of their time looking at dominant individuals. Politics ultimately is all about getting people to notice the politician and to feel good about what they see. Effective leaders keep people's attention because of their ability to grab hold of people's emotions. It should not be surprising that the politician who gets into the press and gets the most coverage has the best chance of winning an election.

This brings to mind the importance of imagery in television and the ability of a candidate to buy his or her way into our living rooms on television. To the extent that television is a tool to shape and reinforce the right image about a candidate, it raises serious questions about whether or not we should limit the amount of coverage a candidate gets during the course of a campaign.[2]

Emotions are captured by images that candidates and political parties portray in commercials. Using the right person or situation juxtaposed with the face of a candidate can go a long way toward capturing votes. For example, in one California Republican commercial, an excerpt from a speech given by Martin Luther King was used to promote a controversial statewide anti-affirmative action initiative. The ad depicted King's vision of a color-blind society in which people would be judged not by the color of their skin but rather by their character. This might have been an effective commercial, but at the same time, it ignited a strong reaction from King's widow. The commercial had juxtaposed King's famous "I have a dream" speech with the proposition on the ballot to end affirmative action in California.[3]

Voters are constantly trying to form opinions about politicians with incomplete information and conflicting images presented to them by many different sources. Take the current campaign finance reform debate going on in the country. How can someone make an intelligent decision on whether the Democrats or Republicans broke the law or on who was honest and who was not? There is a daily barrage of information coming out in the media with new revelations coming through video recordings of the president and other political leaders. Images are created through this process and make it difficult for the average citizen to form accurate perceptions about people.

The challenge to a politician is to convey to voters an ability to be emotionally strong and, at the same time, sensitive. In light of the previous discussion and the difficulty of shaping a political image in a controlled manner, this is not an easy objective to reach, especially considering that different voters look for candidates with different images. We expect our leaders to be compassionate and idealistic and still able to get the job done.[4]

MANUFACTURING PRODUCT IMAGES

Brand images for products represent the overall perceptions of the brands and are formed on the basis of information the consumers have about the brands in addition to their personal experiences with the brands. For example, a consumer who has used Crest toothpaste his whole life will form an image of that brand on the basis of experience in using it as well as knowing that it is supposed to fight tooth decay. Because consumers with positive images of a brand are more likely to purchase it, a major purpose of advertising strategy is to create positive brand images in the minds of consumers.

The image of a brand also is associated with the company that sells it. For example, when General Foods comes out with a new brand of cereal, the image of that new cereal will be influenced by the reputation of General Foods, the corporation.

Small changes in the physical characteristics of a brand can change the image of commonplace products. For example, when Procter & Gamble introduced Cheer with a blue color, consumers associated the color with a cleaner and more effective detergent. When Schweppes first came onto the market in the United States, it could have been positioned as a soft drink or as a mixer. Positioning it as a mixer guided the promotional direction. The use of Commander Whitehead as the dapper Englishman referring to "Schweppervescence" produced an image of prestige for a product category that might otherwise be regarded as commonplace.[5]

Even when competing products and their accompanying services appear to be the same, consumers might perceive differences in the companies or brand images. One of the best examples is Marlboro cigarettes. Although most cigarette brands essentially taste the same and are sold in the same manner, the only way in which to account for Marlboro's extraordinary worldwide market share (approximately 30%) is that Marlboro's "macho cowboy" image struck a responsive chord with most of the cigarette-smoking public. Marlboro was given not just an image but also a personality.[6]

Symbols are very important when establishing and maintaining an image for a product or service. A symbol serves as an information guide to consumers that allows them to associate a complex set of facts and information with a single word or picture. For example, the "doughboy" for Pillsbury symbolizes the quality of the organization. Also, some companies build brands around famous persons, for example, the perfumes Passion (with Elizabeth Taylor) and Uninhibited (with Cher).

So, what exactly is an image? Technically speaking, it is the visual picture that appears in a consumer's mind at the mention of a brand or company name. For example, when McDonald's is mentioned, many people associate that company with a set of golden arches. This is an effective method of simplifying what a company stands for in the minds of consumers. Brand names are used for this purpose, capturing in a single word or two the essence of the company and its products. The name Sony in the electronics industry represents high quality to many people, and the name Southwest in the airline industry represents a company that provides good service at a low price.

Companies work very hard to convey meanings to their brands and their company names through the use of imagery. Most companies rely on mass media advertising to create images for their products. This is true for many service industries, such as insurance and health care, that sell a set of intangible benefits to consumers. This is unlike a company selling a product, which also can use packaging to convey an image for its product. For example, perfume manufacturers are careful to use the right bottles for their products to convey specific images. This is not to suggest that marketers do not have other methods to use to influence the images of their products or services. The choice of a retail outlet through which a product is sold very much influences the image of the product. Furriers, for example, will not sell their products through Wal-Mart Stores to avoid creating the wrong images for their products. Instead, they rely on upscale department stores to sell their furs.

Price is another tool that marketers have at their disposal to create an image. Montblanc fountain pens can sell for hundreds of dollars in some cases, whereas Bic pens usually sell for under a dollar. What does this do to the image of the product? People associate prestige and status with the use of products that are high priced.

MANUFACTURING POLITICAL IMAGES

A citizen's image of a politician consists of the person's subjective understanding of things or what that person likes and dislikes about the politician.

Similar to brand images, political images do not exist apart from the political objects (or the surrounding symbolism) that influence a person's feelings and attitudes about the politician. For example, Clinton's image in the minds of the American people will be influenced by charges that he did something unethical in the Whitewater situation or that he might have sexually harassed Kathleen Willey in the Oval Office. In sum, a politician's image consists of how people perceive the politician based on his or her characteristics, leadership potential, and surrounding messages that are conveyed through the mass media and by word of mouth in everyday communications with friends and family.

In politics, an image is created through the use of visual impressions that are communicated by the candidate's physical presence, media appearances, and experiences and record as a political leader as that information is integrated into the minds of citizens. A candidate's image is affected by endorsements of highly visible people in the country who support him or her. This is no different from the successful endorsements of products by celebrities who help ring up sales for products from beverages (Michael Jordan for Gatorade) to long-distance telephone services (Candice Bergen for Sprint). Similarly in politics, Hollywood stars such as Barbra Streisand and Warren Beatty appeared in front of rallies promoting Clinton during the 1992 campaign. These Hollywood stars have strong followings, and their success rubs off on a candidate when they are seen together on television.

Symbols such as a politician's hairstyle and clothing convey who that person is. For example, a Danish candidate running for office once posed naked with a big sign strategically in front of him that said "No Hidden Agenda." Clearly, the candidate had an impact on the image that voters had of him. In a company, the scientists and engineers in the firm's research and development department must understand the needs of the users of their products. However, customers' needs change over time (as do the attitudes of citizens bombarded by information), and it is incumbent on the company to develop a process aimed at finding ways in which to continue to meet consumer needs. To successfully market a product or president, a clear image must convey a singular message that establishes the product's or president's major virtue. It must convey this message in a distinctive way so that it is not confused with similar messages from competition. Also, it must deliver a message that hits the emotions as well as a person's reasoning. To be effective, an image must be consistently communicated in every message.

A president's competition is vast and varied, and the competition's ability to shape public opinion is far-reaching, thereby impeding on the president's ability to communicate a clear vision to the American people. In addition to people such as Rush Limbaugh and other influential radio talk show hosts, there are congressional leaders, world leaders, interest groups, and others. Because of the tendency of polls to fluctuate, reflecting the fluid mood of the public as a result of the torrent of information and persuasive messages coming out constantly about the president and his actions, it is very difficult for the president to project a clear and cohesive vision to the country when there is instant communication 24 hours a day.

CONSULTANTS AS IMAGE MANUFACTURERS

"We used to create heroes," says Bob Goodman, a veteran media consultant for Republican political candidates. "Not any more, Dad," says his son, Adam, a second-generation media consultant now working with his father—and teaching the older fellow some new tricks. "We're all technocrats now," Adam Goodman says, "reacting to the overnight polls, fighting against shorter and shorter attention spans out there among the voters." "What counts now are tracking polls, focus groups, dial groups, and digital-TV editing machines, and of course the product, a candidate who is able to raise the huge amounts of cash needed to pay for the technology," says James M. Perry, the *Wall Street Journal* reporter who wrote the article in which the Goodmans are quoted. Adam Goodman says, "The older guys [in the consulting business] like being members of the club. They like to hang out in the Senate cloakroom." The younger generation is not interested in belonging to any clubs. So, what works today depends on what the focus groups tell the consultant.[7]

The fact is that today consultants sometimes take the center stage and even determine the issues of a campaign. Technology and money are doing to politics what they have done to sports; they are making them more organized, more professional, more compartmentalized, and less improvised. Politics has become a big and profitable business. Some say that the byproduct of these consultants is cynicism of the electorate and growing armies of people involved in opposition research. Consultants have become more important because they are in a position to help politicians craft winning images that resonate well with citizens over television. As we move from the television era to the Internet era, the expertise necessary to be a successful consultant will have to change.

At the level of overall strategic thinking, the candidates are involved. But when it comes to creating campaign platforms, conducting polls, and setting up promotional strategies, very few candidates get involved. The services offered by consultants include several different activities such as direct mail, fundraising, television and radio spots, issue analysis, and print advertising. The ability to lead during the high-tech age in which we live hinges on the careful selection of the right consultants to run the candidate's campaign, both before and after entering political office.

Results from a nationwide survey of political consultants reveal the increasingly important role they are playing in politics today. Some survey conclusions were that 40% said candidates are neither very involved nor influential when it comes to setting issue priorities; 60% said their candidates were neither very involved nor influential in the day-to-day tactical operation of the electoral campaign; consultants emphasized campaign activities such as fund-raising, advertising strategies, and analysis of voter preferences; consultants believed a winning campaign does not hinge on competence of the candidate, political organization, or the recruitment and use of volunteer workers; the majority of consultants did not provide services such as precinct walking, phone banking or "get out the vote" efforts (all of which are hallmarks of grassroots politicking); major services consultants offer are direct mail, fund-raising, television and radio spots, issue analysis, and print advertising; and the "permanent campaign" means that consultants do not stop consulting after Election Day but rather continue to provide advice on policymaking activities in anticipation of the next reelection campaign and follow their clients into office as formal advisers or political appointees.[8]

This increasing power of consultants is a very serious issue to the general health of our democracy. In the past, when the party bosses were the ones in control, there was a screening process that was put in place to choose these people. Local officials, who themselves were voted into office, were the ones who had positions of power in a campaign. Today, consultants are hired by campaigns in the same way as corporations might hire consultants, that is, based on word-of-mouth recommendations and relative success in the past. Consultants have not been exposed to the public, nor have they been screened by voters in the same way as party officials have been. So, as we become a more market-driven democracy and the power shifts from public officials to hired guns, there is an inherent danger to society that the basis on which candidates are elected will be determined by the ability, both monetarily and otherwise, to hire the right consultant. This is a serious issue and will only be perpetuated by the rising costs to run for public office and the need to hire consultants to manufacture images for politicians.

SELLING THE PRESIDENT'S IMAGE

Some of Clinton's image problems might have had their roots in the culture of his crisis-oriented presidential campaign. From New Hampshire onward, there was one crisis after another, first Gennifer Flowers, then the draft issue, then others. That same mentality has been used in the White House with almost an addiction to crisis.

As Clinton began his presidency, he made one fatal mistake, and that was to change his attitude toward the media. After going through a grueling campaign in which the media gave him a barrage of questions on every facet of his life,

Clinton stepped into his new role as president with a very distant approach to the media. This was visible the morning after the election, when Clinton had the media sitting several hundred feet away from his lectern on the lawn of the governor's mansion. He came out and made a brief speech, took no questions, and kept the media sitting in their seats, finally under his thumb—or so he thought.

This attitude carried on to the White House, with George Stephanopolous closing off the channel of communication between the president and the media, literally closing the door—one that had been kept open by Marlin Fitzwater, Bush's press secretary. Unlike Fitzwater, Stephanopoulos did not schmooze with reporters; instead, he was tight-lipped and always in control. Phone calls would go unreturned. Clinton's poor relationship with the media stagnated for a full 6 months.

On a routine flight to New Hampshire aboard a White House charter, the press corps was served cold food including a croissant, yogurt, and fruit. Previous administrations had served hotcakes and ham omelets on the press plane. Stephanopolous said that this was the same standard of service the press always had received aboard White Hose charters, but the reporters did not buy it. Some have called it the revenge of the White House press corps. Although Clinton had hoped to bypass the Washington, D.C., press corps, that plan did not work.

The media are the retailers who are given the responsibility of presenting the image manufactured for the president to the American people. As with product retailers, if they are not convinced it is a good product, then they will have a hard time selling it in its current package.

Fitzwater was asked early on in Clinton's tenure what he thought about the president's young staff. He responded, "A few more fat old bald men wouldn't hurt the place." Clinton must have been listening. After Clinton muddled through snafus such as "Haircutgate" and "Travelgate," longtime Republican adviser and Clinton friend David Gergen was brought in to take over as director of communications. Gergen was 51 years old when he took over the job from Stephanopoulos, who was 32. Gergen was a tough and tested political pro who had worked for Reagan and Bush. He understood the subtleties of media manipulation, something evident when he helped hatch the idea behind "Reaganomics," a 100-day plan to sell Reagan's economic package to the American people. The strategy centered on a daily routine of giving the media a theme for the day along with a picture that they would take away with them.

A big part of Clinton's image problems early in his tenure as president hinged on the fact that he paid too much attention to detail, such as getting legislation passed, and not enough to the bigger picture—his image as a leader. Clinton was so caught up in his policy wonk mind-set, and so concerned with the specifics of issues of programs he had promised during the campaign, that he forgot that Americans look to the president to be the leader with a vision, someone who is to be respected. Going to town hall meetings to be asked what type of underwear he wears did not help, nor did having his and his wife's characters attacked. The town hall meetings soon came to a halt, at least for a while. What worked as an effective distribution outlet for his ideas during the campaign did not help when it came to governing. He needed to understand that just as taste is not everything to Coca-Cola customers, neither are the specifics of the issues to the American people.

The Clinton presidency has been dogged with a series of controversies that have played a significant role in shaping the image of this president. Beginning with the Flowers announcement in January 1992 that she had a long affair with the president, there has been a constant stream of events that have forced the Clinton White House to go into "image control" mode.

IMAGE DEVELOPMENT EARLY ON

On May 14, 1993, the Clinton administration decided to fire the entire White House travel office and replace it with a Little Rock, Arkansas, travel agency that had handled the Clinton campaign. Of course, this action on the part of a new administration raised eyebrows because of allegations leveled at the administration leading up the dismissal—making calls to the Federal Bureau of Investigation and the Internal Revenue Service, commissioning a questionable audit, and spying on the travel office employees.

What made the firing of the travel office employees even more interesting was the cast of characters involved, which included Harry Thomason, friend, movie maker, and producer of the wonderful clip on Clinton shown at the Democratic Convention in 1992. He was one of a select number of people who had unrestricted access to the White House in the early going. Apparently it was Thomason who, during one of his discussions with Hillary Clinton in the west wing of the White House, set the whole episode in motion. According to press accounts of this affair at the time, the first lady was insistent on getting different people into the travel office. What interest did Thomason have in this affair? The answer could have rested in his part ownership of an air charter service that bid for the White House business.

Travelgate was only one of several "mini" media problems that would follow. Next came "Nannygate," a problem centering on the difficulty of getting congressional approval for some of the president's nominees because they failed to pay social security taxes for their household help. This was a real embarrassment to a White House that seemed to be acting without the careful procedural scrutiny that should have been conducted. The decision of the president to get a $200 haircut on the tarmac of Los Angeles's airport was another media fiasco. There clearly was a feeding frenzy on the president early on in his administration. This was the result of an organization that used the same marketing formula that put its members into the White House to run the administration. The marketing formula did not work, and it changed significantly after these early blunders to pave the way for the successful passing of the president's economic package and the North American Free Trade Agreement.

Clinton even managed to hurt his image while on vacation. When the president took a vacation, he stayed at only the finest luxurious homes loaned to him by some of the country's richest people. This hurt his image in that some argued it raised conflict-of-interest questions. White House aides said that the law does not explicitly state anything about borrowing vacation homes. Presidents before him always have had their own vacation homes. It was interesting to hear how one of his aides put it at the time, saying that it is not that much unlike other families who go to their friends' beach cottages or cabins in the mountains.

Soon after entering the White House, the Clintons stayed in Richard Friedman's estate in Martha's Vineyard, Massachusetts, which comes with horses, swimming, boating, tennis courts, and other nice amenities. For the vacation before that one, they stayed at a three-story mansion with 17 bedrooms, 13 bathrooms, and 3 kitchens in the Coronado, California, vacation home of M. Larry Lawrence, who Clinton named as ambassador to Switzerland. During the summer of 1993, they stayed at the Hilton Head, South Carolina, home of Paul Bob Burge, a businessman from West Virginia. After the 1992 election, they stayed at the oceanfront estate of their producer friends, Harry Thomason and Linda Bloodworth-Thomason, in Santa Barbara, California. Legally, Clinton is required to disclose any gifts worth more than $250, but he has not listed the vacation retreats as gifts, some valued at $4,500 a day if they were rented. The point here is not the specifics but rather the image left with the American people. The Clinton marketing team did not pay enough attention early on to the overall image and paid too much attention to the details of getting bills passed.

If we were to compare Clinton to other modern-day presidents, then we would see that the fights between the presidents and their enemies were waged on ideological grounds (e.g., Nixon as the rabid anti-Communist, Harry Truman as being soft on communism). However, in the case of Clinton, the attacks seem to have been based on personal grounds, reflecting a serious image problem centered on his character. Part of this could be because the United States did not face any serious economic or foreign crises when Clinton entered office, making it difficult to make the presidency "larger than life" and leaving pundits to comment only on the man and his habits.

THE LAUNCH OF NEW COKE AND
HEALTH CARE REFORM

Health care reform presented a different marketing challenge to Clinton's image, one that many incorrectly thought would either make or break his chances for reelection in 1996. The problem with the Clinton administration's launch of health care is best explained by looking at the launch for New Coke back in 1985. The parallels are strikingly similar.

The Coca-Cola Company, after close to 100 successful years, dropped its original formula Coke for a new one. In place of it would come New Coke, with a sweeter and smoother taste. At first, New Coke sold well, but then sales seemed to start dropping. Angry consumers starting writing and calling the company to complain, and protests and class action suits threatened the company unless the company brought back its old formula. Some business analysts even predicted that New Coke would be the "Edsel of the Eighties." Only 2 months after the introduction of the product, the Coca-Cola Company reintroduced the original Coke, called Coke Classic, sold side by side in supermarkets next to New Coke. However, by the end of 1985, Coke Classic was outselling New Coke in supermarkets by nearly two to one. By mid-1986, the company's two largest fountain accounts, McDonald's and Kentucky Fried Chicken, returned to serving Coke Classic. So, why was New Coke introduced, and why did it fail? Are there any lessons for being a leader in the 1990s and beyond? Many analysts blame poor marketing research as the cause of the failure.

In response to losing market share to Pepsi, based in part on the successful "Pepsi Challenges" (a series of televised taste tests showing consumers preferring the sweeter taste of Pepsi), the Coca-Cola Company began the largest new product research project in the company's history. It spent more than 2 years and $4 million on research before arriving at its new formula. It actually conducted some 200,000 taste tests, with close to 30,000 on the final formula alone. Research indicated that New Coke would be a winner, and it was introduced with a lot of fanfare.

Looking back, the company's research was too narrowly focused, looking only at taste without looking at how consumers felt about dropping the old Coke and replacing it with a new version. The research consisted of mainly "blind" comparisons, which did not take into account the total product—the name, history, packaging, image, and the like. To many people, Coke stood for hot dogs and apple pie, almost like an American institution. That deep emotional connection to the roots of the brand were not measured, and to many consumers the symbolic meaning was more important than taste.[9]

In an effort to pass his health care reform package, Clinton relied on a familiar "war room" strategy to market health care reform. This included extensive polling to determine what voters were looking for in a plan, several electronic town hall meetings to sell the plan, and a media campaign to compete with the "Harry and Louise" image campaign waged against his plan by the insurance lobby. Clinton's strategists realized that the reason their plan had gone down in popularity was not due to the content but rather was due to the lack of a simple message to communicate the essence of the plan to the American people. Subsequently, Clinton altered his marketing strategy in town hall meetings and press releases to present a simple message targeted to the 58 million people who were not covered by health insurance. In a word, the marketing of this plan failed because of the inability of the president's strategists to use the right image or to put the right "face" on the package they were selling. Or, in contrast to the highly successful Harry and Louise campaign, the president never came up with a face, whereas his opponents did.

Earlier in Clinton's term, internal polling revealed that the health care sales pitch that was used initially was not working. Essentially, the president had admitted that the public was confused about his plan. This confusion only worked to help his opponents, from Limbaugh to Bob Dole, who had been battering away at the president's ideas. To avoid the confusion, the president altered his message (like a good marketer) and eliminated references to "universal coverage," "insurance purchasing alliances," and "employer mandates." In their place were phrases such as "guaranteed private insurance," "real insurance reform," and "health benefits guaranteed at work." The new phrases were test marketed by Stanley Greenberg, who discovered that the president's plan won stronger approval ratings when the terms used did not have as much health care jargon in them.

To communicate better with the American people, Clinton reduced the complex subject of health care to a few simple red, white, and blue charts, which were interpreted with homespun humor and a distinct anti-Washington tone. As opposed to a health care blitz, the new sales effort put into gear in the spring of 1994 resembled a traveling seminar in which 1,300 pages of legislation were condensed into bite-size messages for the masses. The president hoped that repetition and simplicity would revitalize his plan after thousands of presidential words and speeches, press conferences and briefings had not done so. His own people felt as if it had been a failure of salesmanship and communication, that is, good substance with a bad message that failed because of the inability of the president to get his message across.

In fact, it seemed as if the president was acting like there was an election just around the corner. With colorful balloons, hoisted signs, and an enthusiastic crowd of people yelling at the top of their lungs, here came Clinton. With his voice turned up in campaign-style volume to the delight of the crowds, the president traveled around the country trying to sell his health plan. The marketing of Clinton's health care package mushroomed into a full-scale campaign, complete with all the physical trappings and rhetoric that running for modern office has come to imply.[10]

Clinton failed on health care because the package was too partisan, was not marketed properly, was out of touch with market changes taking place as it was being developed, and was too complex and because the insurance lobby's response with the Harry and Louise commercials was very effective. In the end, the American people were not persuaded that the changes proposed by the president would leave them with a health care system better than the one they currently had. Old habits are hard to change.

WHITEWATER: OLD PROBLEMS, NEW IMAGES

The Whitewater affair presented another big challenge to the Clinton administration from an image management perspective. On the one hand, it is a problem that has threatened his entire presidency, with the possibility in the first term that it might make him a lame duck president.

The affair clearly has left the president in the precarious position of defending his wife and, at the same time, facing embarrassing questions on how an initial investment of $1,000 mushroomed into close to a $100,000 gain in only a few years. The gain paints a picture of the president and his wife as part of the "greedy 1980s crowd."

A few couriers of the Rose Law Firm in Little Rock said that Hillary Clinton had asked them on two occasions in the summer of 1992 to go to the governor's mansion to pick up boxes of records that they were to shred. Later that year, eight more boxes were shredded. In January 1994, partners from the Rose Law Firm admitted that they did, in fact, shred files that they previously had said were unrelated to Whitewater.

Whitewater presented the president with some particular problems during some of his town hall meetings when he was attacked about his character. In one town hall meeting in Charlotte, North Carolina, that was televised in nine states, Clinton defended his trustworthiness, assuring a woman who said the Whitewater controversy had tarred his credibility: "You will not be ashamed of what I do as president."[11] Clinton defended his money-losing Whitewater investment and his wife's big gains in the cattle futures market, saying that in all his years in public life, he never had been accused of scandal or abuse of power in public office. Clinton's Whitewater story was that he lost money on Whitewater and was cooperating with investigators, that he fully disclosed his tax returns for that period, that his wife had released details of her commodities trading, and that the trading was legal.

With time as the ultimate acid test, and after having several government-appointed panels looking into the affair, nothing had been found that pointed to illegalities on the part of either the president or his wife when this book went to press.

THE FIRST LADY'S IMAGE

Soon after Clinton entered the White House, Hillary Clinton sat around a table with senators from the Senate Finance Committee, a group that would be critical to the passage of the health care reform legislation, and as it is told by Lawrence O'Donnell, Jr., the committee's chief of staff,

> Mrs. Clinton came into the room, and she opened the discussion at about [4:25] in the afternoon. We were about [18] minutes into it when she stopped—I remember, I looked at the clock. And what I had just heard were the most perfectly composed, perfectly punctuated sentences, growing into paragraphs, in the most perfect, fluid presentation about what our problems in this field were and what we could do about them. . . . And then she held her position in the face of questioning by these senators around the table, many of whom know a great deal about the subject. And she was more impressive than any Cabinet member who has sat in that chair.[12]

That was early on in the administration. Since that time, the first lady's image outside the White House changed dramatically. So, what happened?

Hillary Clinton's intellect had amazed members of Congress from the beginning. Let us not forget that she was a first-rate lawyer with a reputation as a person with a fine analytical mind. But who knew that she would be the best marketing asset the president had early on? When she would visit members of Congress, along came the photographer, snapping pictures of her along with the congresspersons and members of their staff. Several days later, in the mail would come autographed photographs.

The comment from one congressman, as retold in an article in *The New Yorker*, was,

> All these egomaniacs—the notion that the first lady would come to their office! And these were more than courtesy calls. They were so scripted and focused, she could have been working for the CIA [Central Intelligence Agency]. These were intelligence-gathering meetings, not chit-chat. When she visited my boss, the visit was scheduled for a half hour, and she spent an hour and a half. They talked about health care, his home state, kids—everything. She was trying to figure out what these people were about.[13]

When the time came to testify at hearings of the Senate and House committees, Hillary Clinton had a dossier on everyone, interweaving into her comments personal asides about each of the members sitting on the panel.

IMAGERY AND PRESIDENTIAL CAMPAIGNS

A candidate's image often is defined from relatively minor incidents that the media seem to hang onto. For example, Carter never was able to shake the story by *Playboy* magazine in which he said that he has lust in his heart. The press never let go of Johnson's displaying his surgical scar or of Nixon's walking along a beach in his wingtip shoes. In a similar way, a president's image can be tarnished by his Hollywood connections early on. For example, Billy Crystal was briefed by Cabinet secretaries early in Clinton's tenure. This did not look good. Likewise, Bush was affected by Michael Jackson moonwalking through the White House.[14]

The 1996 presidential election left us with some of the most memorable images ever created by a set of candidates. Perhaps the most memorable and most important is the image of Clinton. The question is which image he portrayed to which segment of voters. For example, as soon as he would go below the Mason-Dixon line, a transformation would take place. His walk would become less stiff and not nearly as formal, almost as if he was not the president anymore. He seemed to grin more when he was in the South, almost casting himself into the role of a "good ol' boy" who fit right in with his environment by dropping his G's and flattening his I's. He also grew more nostalgic and began to speak with more colorful words. In a word, he became southern. It was something that southerners could spot immediately, and the president knew it. Clinton has an amazing capacity to fit in with whomever he is with.[15]

Another amazing transformation that took place during the campaign was that of Dole, from political insider to political outsider almost as quickly as it would take Clark Kent to turn from newspaper reporter into Superman simply by putting on a costume. Dole effectively did the same thing when he opted for open-neck shirts over gray pin-striped suits with ties.

For Dole, the hope was that the American people were looking for someone who was not too slick. In fact, Dole was the first to admit that during campaign appearances, telling his audience members that they were not going to get the slickest candidate with him. For Dole to convey that he was real, he had to do things that in reality made him look artificial. This never was more revealing than when Dole walked off the plane soon after announcing he was leaving the Senate in a Johnny Carson sport coat, cream-colored khakis, and loafers with tassels. As Dole walked down off the plane, he looked extremely self-conscious. Most interesting was that even with his new casual look, he still wore cufflinks. Dole tried to look the part of just an ordinary guy, a real American to whom everybody could relate—except himself.[16]

Images of Clinton and Dole sometimes did not seem to fit the men. For example, there was Dole as he took a short vacation on the beaches of Florida.

Trying to look younger than his 72 years, there he was, walking along the shore of a Florida beach, dressed in short pants and a summer shirt, trying to look the part of just another vacationer. It just did not seem to be the Dole who the country had come to know. Similarly, Clinton hardly looked the part of the seasoned war veteran when he was commemorating the 50th anniversary of the Normandy invasion and was pictured walking along the beaches. Unfortunately for him, he does not have the legs of a John F. Kennedy, and the imagery did not work.

During the 1996 presidential election, we saw Dole touring a flag factory, clearly with the idea of creating a patriotic image. We also saw Lamar Alexander wearing his ever-present flannel shirt, conveying the image of the "laid-back candidate." These types of image manipulation techniques are not new. Calvin Coolidge wore an Indian war bonnet to lighten up his image. Teddy Roosevelt made sure that one of his campaign posters had a picture of him charging up San Juan Hill. Andrew Jackson's enemies smeared him using stenciled hand-bills picturing him with shapes of coffins representing soldiers under his command. Daniel Webster tried to transform himself into a log cabin populist, even though most saw him as a Washington insider. Carter always was seen in his cardigan sweater, looking plain and simple for the people.

During the 1996 campaign, Clinton was pictured by his opponents as too slick, and Dole was painted as nasty and mean. The serious focus on character is not new, but with the presence of television images in our living rooms from morning 'til night, the negative campaigning has turned off many voters. Close to 20% of the American voters continue to be uninformed and uninvolved in politics.[17]

Images also are created when candidates are accused of misdeeds by their opponents, and as a result, innuendo leaves impressions in voters' minds that become difficult to change. For example, Dole was accused of being a nicotine pusher who did not care about the effects of smoke on children. Clinton was accused of pandering to everyone just to get their votes. Accusations are not new in politics. Thomas Jefferson was accused of taking one of his slaves as a mistress and even of planning to outlaw Christianity. Lincoln was alleged to have had an illegitimate daughter with one of his own slaves. One has to begin to question why product manufacturers do not engage in the same type of negative campaigning. The answer lies in the law.

First, the Federal Trade Commission does not have any jurisdiction over political commercials as it does over product commercials or advertisements. In other words, virtually anything can be said by a politician, and the politician does not have to be held accountable. Second, consumers are far more interested in buying products than in voting for candidates, so negative campaigning to get the attention of voters is not as necessary for product marketers.

The image of Dole, for most voters, was that of the Senate leader and deal maker for most of his career. He also had the image of a dedicated soldier who, wounded and in the hospital for a long time, left a hero. A video made for the Republican National Convention depicted Dole's visit to his hometown of Russell, Kansas, where he was greeted as a Horatio Alger-like figure. At the convention, Dole's wife, Elizabeth, carefully crafted the image of the man she knows so well as she told the story of his life. She described him as a small boy who grew up poor but rich in terms of values handed down to him from his family. During the videotape, Dole is seen embracing one of the nurses who helped rehabilitate him after World War II.

For the tape, an African American family from Russell was included. The person chosen, Natonya Cullors (a Democrat), said herself that she was chosen because of her status as an unwed mother and welfare recipient and because of the color of her skin. "It was done for the cameras because we are Black," Cullors said. This type of image manipulation and stage management was nothing new in the 1996 campaign. Clinton, in his videotape 4 years earlier as the "man from Hope," introduced the political world to the mastery of Hollywood through his friends and producers, the Thomasons, who made the videotape.[18,19]

In 1992 in Philadelphia, Clinton's people engaged in image manufacturing and stage management by taping a spot in front of Geno's, a cheesesteak restaurant frequented by blue-collar workers. Here, the idea was to create the image of Clinton as one of the regular guys. In Arkansas, the same scenario was carried out, this time in front of Harvey's, a little country store famous for the barbecue pork sandwiches it serves on Saturday afternoons. Again, the idea was to depict Clinton as just one of the guys.

When Dole painted a picture of himself as a war hero, he was referring to Kennedy's own experience in the military and, in effect, was using Kennedy's image to create one for himself. This strategy is similar to one used by Carter's pollster, Pat Caddell, who tried to convince both Gary Hart and Joseph Biden that they could improve their images by associating themselves with the 1960s, when rock music and war protesters were prevalent. Both Hart and Biden failed with that type of imagery. This is a generational appeal, and one that Clinton used effectively by turning his youth into an image of strength and vigor. Kennedy did the same as a post-Dwight Eisenhower candidate, looking and sounding much younger than his older predecessor in the White House.[20]

The person who perfected the art of image crafting is Michael Deaver, Reagan's assistant. Deaver's strategy for Reagan was to emphasize family, neighborhood, and peace. Every stop that Reagan made had to have one of the three as a backdrop. Deaver also put a great deal of stock in lighting. He thought that lighting made the difference in a visual shot of Reagan. In fact, Dole's top campaign people confessed to seeking Deaver's advice. To Deaver, the visual was everything because, according to his thinking, people perceive more from visuals than from information.[21]

CONCLUSION

Constructing political meanings and realities out of the myriad of messages coming out of a political campaign is becoming very difficult for the average citizen. It is information that is paid for and the symbols that a politician creates that are used by voters to form attitudes and voting preferences. Political meaning is conveyed through the media and their interpretations and perceptions. At the core of candidate-manufactured images is the attempt to manipulate and control media coverage to paint the best possible television face for a candidate and, at the same time, to mold an image consistent with the appeal that the candidate wants to use to win over voters.

In effect, the media creates a constructed reality for the voters, based on both the substance and the images they convey. The media intensify previously held emotional beliefs of voters by framing, highlighting, and attributing responsibility for particular events or outcomes to certain politicians. Voters then take in all of this information and attach new meanings to it based on their own perceptual filtering systems and desires. This is not dissimilar to the process that goes on for the marketing of any product or service, with the key difference being that the manufacturer has more control over conveying the meaning it wants than does a politician, who must rely on the media to serve as information disseminator. Ultimately, it is critical for a politician to understand how voters perceive the politician relative to his or her candidacy and to use the information that is generated from marketing research to reinforce or reposition the meaning that voters attach to a candidacy.[22]

Just as Reagan was the "Teflon president" to which nothing bad could stick, Clinton has created an image of himself as the "Velcro president" to which just about everything sticks, if only for a while. According to Lichtman and DeCell in *The 13 Keys to the Presidency,* for a major scandal to diminish the president's ability to govern, "the wrongdoing has to bring discredit upon the president himself, calling into question his personal integrity, his judgment as chief executive, or at least his faithfulness in upholding the law."[23] Even with the allegations of the president's sexual encounters with Lewinsky and Willey, the president's approval ratings suggest that none of the allegations leveled against him have diminished his ability to drive public opinion.

One of the most telling news conferences the president has held during his tenure as president was the first one that followed the breaking of the Lewinsky story, where Clinton was asked whether his moral leadership had been impaired by the allegations that had been leveled at him. Clinton responded by saying that his reputation might have been damaged but that his character never would be affected. Herein lies the challenge to leaders in all democracies—the ability to manufacture images of themselves that reveal only the positive sides of their characters, regardless of how damaged their reputations might be.

NOTES

1. McGeary, J. (1996, December 16). Mix and match. *Time,* pp. 29-33.

2. McDonald, K. (1996, January 5). Scholarship. *Chronicle of Higher Education,* pp. A7-A14.

3. Haynes, D. V. (1996, October 25). King speech in GOP ad sparks furor. *Chicago Tribune,* sec. 1, p. 10.

4. Renshon, S. A. (1996). *The psychological assessment of the president.* New York: New York University Press.

5. Assael, H. (1984). *Consumer behavior and marketing action.* Boston: Kent.

6. Kotler, P. (1994). *Marketing management* (7th ed.). Englewood Cliffs, NJ: Prentice Hall.

7. Perry, J. M. (1994, January 10). Young guns: A second generation of political handlers outduels forebears. *Wall Street Journal,* pp. A1, A7.

8. Dellios, H. (1994, June 21). Unflappable prosecutor may face no-win situation. *Chicago Tribune,* sec. 1, p. 15.

9. See Kotler (Note 6).

10. Neikirk, W. (1994, April 9). Selling health plan: Clinton '94 campaign. *Chicago Tribune,* sec. 1, pp. 1, 10.

11. Associated Press. (1994, April 6). At town hall gathering, Clinton defends integrity. *Chicago Tribune,* sec. 1, p. 10.

12. Bruck, C. (1994, May 30). Hillary the pol. *The New Yorker,* p. 58.

13. See Bruck (Note 12, p. 59).

14. Carlson, M., Painton, P., & Kramer, M. (1993, May 31). Shear dismay. *Time,* pp. 20-23.

15. Neikirk, W. (1996b, October 25). Clinton's message with a twang. *Chicago Tribune,* sec. 1, p. 16.

16. Dowd, M. (1996, May 20). Dole's bid to seem down- home needs a dose of theatrics. *Chicago Tribune,* sec. 1, p. 15.

17. Neikerk, W. (1996a, May 26). Campaigns breed elements of character and caricatures. *Chicago Tribune,* sec. 1, p. 6.

18. Madigan, C. (1996, August 15). Dole at last wears GOP mantle: Candidate called man of honor. *Chicago Tribune,* sec. 1, pp. 1, 26.

19. Hardy, T. H., & Madigan, C. (1996, August 16). Dole to America: You can trust me. *Chicago Tribune,* sec. 1, pp. 1, 22.

20. Krauthammer, C. (1995b, February 24). In his presidential bid, Dole can capitalize on JFK. *Chicago Tribune,* sec. 1, p. 15.

    21. Shalt, R. (1997, July 1). Dr. Spin: It's all in the lighting. *Gentleman's Quarterly,*
p. 19.
    22. Miller, A. H., & Gronbeck, B. E. (Eds.). (1994). *Presidential campaigns and
American self-images.* Boulder, CO: Westview.
    23. Lichtman, A. J., & DeCell, K. (1990). *The 13 keys to the presidency.* Lanham,
MD: Madison Books.

7

The Permanent Campaign

A government is based on public opinion and must keep in step with what public opinion decides, which considers and calculates everything.
— Napoleon Bonaparte, letter, November 25, 1803

In *The Prince,* Machiavelli described the successful leader as someone able to combine the strength of a lion and the cunning of a fox. In today's more complicated world, his perception still holds true, yet one also needs deliberate and delicate balancing of several approaches to create purposeful, effective leadership.

Remember the Edsel? That was the car on which Ford lost $350 million and went down in history as perhaps the greatest of all marketing failures. Texas Instruments lost $660 million before it pulled out of the home computer business. RCA lost $575 million on its videodisc players.[1] Each of these companies failed despite excellent research and development that helped to create a superior product. Each failed because consumers in the marketplace did not want to buy the product. Furthermore, each of these companies could not effectively compete in a marketplace where superior products existed at lower prices.

The Concorde supersonic passenger jet failed despite its advantages. The biggest advantage it advertised, a time-saving way of traveling, was eliminated with the travel delays at either end of a trip. This was in addition to the public policy problems caused because of the noise pollution it was creating. Despite new technology and sharp design both inside and outside the jet, the concept failed because passengers did not gain enough utility for the higher price.[2]

Just as companies must adapt to the forces of the marketplace once they finish perfecting the manufacturing process, so too must a candidate adapt from the "campaign marketplace" to the "governing marketplace" to be a successful politician. After entering the White House, a president must understand that there is a whole new host of challenges and changes in the marketplace. The campaign is the period during which the presidential candidate develops his campaign platform, adjusts and refines his image, tests out both, and arrives at a contract with the American people that he promises to keep after he enters the White House. However, once a candidate wins the election, it is time to deliver, a time when voters look to the president to carry out his promises.

Today, the governing process has turned into a permanent marketing campaign,[3] with a reliance on polling to monitor citizen reaction to various presidential initiatives, electronic town hall meetings to disseminate the president's message, computers to analyze the electorate's needs and wants, facsimile machines to distribute information to key opinion leaders, cable television to go direct to the citizens, focus groups to help craft and refine the president's image, "800" telephone numbers to solicit donations, and every other imaginable technological advance and marketing tool that a president can use to drive public opinion. This is the state of politics as we enter the new millennium—government by public opinion.

CHANGES IN THE
MARKETING FORMULA

The marketing challenge to a candidate who enters the White House is enormous because of several changes that take place in the marketplace. First, the needs of the American people change after a candidate enters office. During a campaign, voters are more interested in the personality of the candidate, whether he is believable, and whether he would be an effective leader. Once in office, if the nation is at peace, then the needs of citizens become more rational. As citizens, people are most concerned about paying their bills and raising their families. Their needs are centered around their children and their homes. If a president is able to keep interest rates down, keep American soldiers at home in peace, and maintain a semblance of order in his own house, then the needs of the American people always will be satisfied. Only after looking into their own affairs will people look to a president to deliver on the promises he made during the campaign.

Second, the marketplace broadens significantly after a candidate enters office. The competitive environment will now include many different constituencies whose lives will be affected by the decisions the president makes. Many of these constituencies will have a formalized organizational structure that represents their interests in Washington, D.C. If one adds to these groups the radio talk show hosts, media, pollsters, corporate lobbyists and ambassadors from countries around the world, all of whom want the president's ear, then it should become obvious why a president has to rely on marketing to effectively respond to the needs and wants of these different groups of people.

Third, the product changes dramatically. Instead of candidates talking about their ideas on how to change the country, leaders have to market programs and policies and show results. Promises made during a campaign must be delivered in the form of programs. Moving the campaign into the White House brings with it a reliance on a new "team" to run the country. This is a marketing management issue that centers on the tactics of planning and control within the White House. The image of the president also has to be reengineered to reflect the broader marketplace to which he is selling his ideas. This inevitably will put pressure on the president to manufacture a new image that is positioned more toward the center of the political spectrum.

Fourth, a leader must drive public opinion on a more permanent basis, not just respond to it in the heat of a political campaign. During a campaign, the candidates use polling and marketing research to define the needs of voters and then respond to them by presenting campaign platforms and images of themselves that look and sound appealing. Once in office, a president sometimes has to go against public opinion. A good marketer anticipates the needs in the marketplace and then develops products or services to satisfy those needs. A president cannot afford to respond to the ebb and flow of public opinion in a "knee jerk" fashion. The president must articulate his vision to the American people and convince them to follow his lead. Keep in mind that it becomes impossible to drive public opinion if the president does not have a handle on the thinking of the American people, hence the preoccupation with polls.

A "permanent campaign" markets all the policies—including unpopular ones—in an attempt to sell and effectively implement the long-term vision of the president and his party. Government by public opinion forces presidents to rely on marketing to be successful.

MAKING THE SWITCH

At the highest levels of Bill Clinton's White House, the consensus was that running the Oval Office was like running a campaign. According to Hillary Clinton, "I think you have to run a campaign for policy just like you do for elections." She was convinced that she and the president had to "sell" their ideas and policies to the public and Congress and inevitably were stuck in campaign mode. She believed that the barrage of attacks against her husband centered not on him personally but rather on his ideas. The first lady knew that she and the president were fighting an entrenched establishment that forced them into this permanent campaign throughout his presidency.[4]

Many of the same people who ran Clinton's first campaign came with him to the White House, a common trend in politics. Although campaign-tested and loyal to Clinton, several aides were young, untested consultants who naively tried to apply the same marketing formula they had used successfully during the campaign to governing during his first term. This forced the permanent campaign mentality onto the strategic operations of the White House and, in so doing, proved to be one of the failings of Clinton's leadership style early on. Running the White House like a presidential campaign does not allow the president to make the necessary organizational and management changes needed for an effective operation. Going directly to the people with town hall meetings and talk shows might work during the campaign but will present a whole host of new difficulties when used to run the country.

MARKETING MISSTEPS EARLY ON

We can point to some self-inflicted wounds the president incurred by concentrating on a controversial issue such as gays in the military and by experiencing some early setbacks such as "Nannygate," "Travelgate," and "Haircutgate" (his $200 haircut). In marketing, we call these "marketing missteps" or mistakes a company makes as a result of a poor execution of strategy. Even in the face of resistance that built up against his health care reform proposals shortly after they were introduced to the American people, Clinton seemed resistant to change and to the type of flexibility needed to implement a marketing strategy successfully. In other words, a good marketer adapts to the forces in the marketplace, something Clinton did not do early in his tenure.

The interest level in politics and the White House drops off significantly after the campaign is over, leaving tremendous power in the hands of the media to shape the president's image through the snippets of information shown on the evening news each night. Citizens become passive "information processors" once the candidate wins office and do not seek out information as aggressively as they might during the heat of a campaign. The people driving Clinton's marketing campaign early on lost control over the image they had manufactured so well during the campaign.

After Clinton's first 100 days in office, his approval ratings looked rather mixed, as 43% approved of how he was handling the economy, 40% approved of what he was doing about the budget deficit, 34% approved of how he was handling taxes, 53% approved of his management of foreign affairs, 55% supported his economic plan, 63% had favorable opinions of him, 61% gave Hillary Clinton a favorable rating, 64% thought the president cared about the needs of the American people, 61% thought he was honest and trustworthy, and 61% thought he was tough enough to do the job. These last three statistics certainly were good enough to keep him in good standing with the American people.[5]

After the first 100 days, we saw a president who was torn between being a policy wonk and being a politician, the key marketing transition he needed to make to be effective. On any one day, he zig-zagged between each. He seemed to be torn between doing what his own sense said he should do and taking the course he knew would increase his standing in the polls. This same "tug and pull" has affected every recent president. For example, Ronald Reagan, with his great political skills, focused on delivering a basic message to voters and left the policy details to others. On the other hand, Jimmy Carter focused on policy but often was unable to gauge the political fallout of his actions; he was not adept at understanding how politics flowed from good policy.

After 5 months in office, Clinton's approval ratings were not very impressive when compared to those of other modern-day presidents. Clinton was at 36%, compared to approval ratings of 59% for Reagan, 63% for Carter, and 70% for George Bush at the like periods in their terms.[6]

In general, Clinton's problem centered on his inability to project a clear vision of what he stood for. Unlike other modern-day presidents, Clinton was unsuccessful at separating the big picture from the daily tug and pull of politics. Compared to other modern-day presidents, Clinton was missing a vision on which to base his message. For example, Reagan, with his great political skills, delivered a basic message to voters and left the policy details to others. Carter focused on policy but often misjudged the political fallout of his actions.

Another reason behind Clinton's marketing problems early on were his efforts to run the nation as a majority president, which he was not. Minority presidents, by definition, have to govern from the center, pushing the American voters slowly inward from the extremes of the political spectrum. Clinton had difficulty in doing this.

Clinton also needed to maintain a key ingredient that made him successful in the campaign, and that was *flexibility*. This meant letting go of an initiative if it did not get up enough steam, for example, his proposed health care legislation. At the core of marketing thought is the importance that is placed on adapting a product to the needs and wants of the consumers in the marketplace and not forcing a product onto people. In effect, the president was trying to force a product onto unwilling customers.

There is, of course, the danger of relying too heavily on the polls. It can give way to an unprincipled acquiescence to public opinion. This is something that Bush found out, but Clinton promised to be different. In fact, Clinton, the good marketer that he is, promised the American people that he would not let the whims of public sentiment determine his policies. Some have accused the president of relying on focus groups to watch him and then register their reactions during his speeches.

However, some of those close to Clinton, such as strategist Paul Begala, have argued that the president did not let polls dictate policy but instead relied on them simply as feedback (as opposed to direction-setting tools). According to the president's advisers, polls are used to tell them whether what the president is communicating is effective or not. Given that Clinton won the presidency with less than one half of the popular vote, it is obvious why there is this pressure to please the electorate and to consult the polls for more than simple feedback. "This administration uses polls as feedback, not to chart a course," Begala protests. "Polls tell us whether what we're doing to communicate is working."[7]

On May 10, 1993, Begala and Republican media consultant Roger Ailes were on ABC's *Nightline* program (with Ted Koppel) to discuss Clinton's first few months in the White House. At one point in the program, Ailes said, "Basically, Bill Clinton got elected saying he wanted to go to Washington and fix things. . . . He's been there [2] months, and now he doesn't want to be in Washington." Begala retorted, "Bill Clinton's strength is his outside game. . . . He's always going to be someone who's better with the American people than he is with the Beltway politicians and pundits." Ailes shot back, "The translation of that is . . . you heard one of his top advisers say he's lousy at governing but very good at campaigning."[8]

LEARNING ON THE JOB

During Clinton's first 2 years in office, the media did not let even the smallest incident go by unnoticed. They began with the exposure of Clinton's fascination with "Kennedy-like" behavior patterns such as his warm embrace of Hollywood. Some of Clinton's closest allies during the campaign, Hollywood producers such as Harry Thomason and his wife, had to reduce their visibility because of the exposure they were getting in the press—including office space in the White House for Thomason. This was the beginning of the power struggle within the White House that would raise its ugly head for the Clintons in the future, with Hillary Clinton firing most of the kitchen staff and some of the ushers who still were carrying on communications with the Bushes. These events, all of them seemingly minor, reflected a very inexperienced White House staff around a president who seemed to be out of his league in Washington.

On July 8, 1993, Clinton's top consultants delivered a one-page memo to Clinton's chief of staff titled *Proposal for Coordinating Strategy and Message.* In it, there was a proposal for setting up the "PIT" (as in stock exchange pit) in Room 180 of the Old Executive Office Building. Anyone who referred to it as the "war room" would be fined $10. Roger Altman was chosen to head up the group, with representatives from several agencies and sections of the White House also to be included. Each day, the vice president and chief of staff met with several Cabinet members and top consultants in a morning meeting. Eventually, it did become known as the war room, and the fight for the economic plan early in Clinton's first term became another "campaign," the first of many that would crop up during his presidency.[9]

The management style used soon after entering the White House was questionable. In each department of government, veterans of his successful presidential campaign were crossing swords with policy experts who had formal titles as Cabinet secretaries. The president was finding it difficult to choose among them. This was in great contrast to the Clinton campaign, when each message was crisp and sharp, and his opponents' messages often were vague. Initially in his term, the opposite occurred.

Another explanation is that much of his campaign machine had been dismantled, with James Carville, the genius who directed the campaign, being too busy with his own ventures and with much of his top staff being only part-time advisers to the president. To alleviate this problem, Clinton gave more authority to his political people such as political director Rahm Emanuel, who was given control of intergovernmental relations.

Clinton entered the White House with one of the most detailed and ambitious agendas in modern history, with universal health coverage as the key point. He ended his first year on a downbeat, with nagging questions about his personal life and investments of the past. Although his pledge of universal health care coverage was pursued, other promises were dropped such as a middle class tax cut and a college program to pay back loans. He stuck to his vow to shift the White House focus to domestic affairs. But even this backfired with some stumbling on foreign affairs, especially in trouble spots such as Bosnia and Somalia as well as a flip-flop on the policy toward Haitian boat people.

Clinton's management style was criticized because of a lack of planning. Instead of pacing the work with a sense of discipline, there seemed to be this great rush at the end, prompting deals and compromises to win support. In fact, Clinton was described by one White House staffer as someone who likes to lay down in front of trains and then get up and out of the way at the very last moment. Clinton's management style definitely had a crisis orientation that did not serve him well early in his tenure as president.

David Gergen helped Clinton to whittle down broad-ranging issues into a clear message of the day. More important, Gergen represented an adviser who would be nonpartisan and a pragmatist who embodied the centrist position on which Clinton campaigned. This helped to eradicate the perception that Clinton was a far left-winger, but only after several embarrassing incidents that did not help the president's image with his various constituencies.

THE MARKETING MANTRA:
DON'T PROMISE WHAT YOU CAN'T DELIVER

After his first year in office, Clinton's track record on major pledges definitely was mixed. He promised to cut the federal budget deficit by half and, in fact, narrowly carried out his economic plan. He promised to reduce the middle class tax burden, a goal he abandoned early in his first year after discovering that the deficit was worse than he had thought. He did, however, keep his promise to increase taxes on the affluent and to give a tax break to the poor. He promised to reform the political system, with legislation to revamp campaign finance rules and to stop the revolving door between government and lobbying firms. This was stalled after the first year. He promised to end the ban on homosexuals in the military. However, after having confrontations with the military, the White House agreed to a policy of "don't ask, don't tell, don't pursue," a compromise criticized by both sides.

Clinton promised to stimulate job creation, and although he was unable to fund any big jobs program, he was successful in passing the North American Free Trade Agreement (NAFTA) and, therefore, was successful in creating domestic work. He promised to create a national service program, which Congress enacted by giving educational awards of up to $4,725 a year to students who perform community service. This, however, was much smaller in scale than the program once envisioned and was limited to 100,000 participants. Finally, he promised to fight crime, and he did succeed in signing the "Brady Bill" (to control handgun purchases) and later passed a crime bill during his second year.[10]

Clinton's consultants always kept an eye toward 1996. In fact, Stan Greenberg, Clinton's pollster, knew all along that any broken promises from the campaign would have lasting repercussions on the president's reelection chances. However, from a marketing perspective, it was short-sighted on the part of the Clinton administration to think that every promise could be fulfilled or not to understand that a good marketer must be flexible and responsive to the events of the day. The most damaging finding in Greenberg's research was that Clinton had lost his message of putting people first, one that had resonated so clearly in the ears of voters during the campaign. Still, Greenberg relied on the use of focus groups to help chart the course in the political waters of Washington.

A good marketer captures the interest and curiosity of the target market before the product enters the marketplace. Early in his presidency, Clinton did exactly that, raising expectations of the consumers or, in this case, the voters. However, he also did not deliver on what he promised, and this is something that can kill the best of products. In trying to remanufacture his image to a centrist position, he tried to rearrange the nation's priorities. Because of his unwillingness to take the steps to cut the deficit even more than he did, he sort of backed himself into a corner, limiting his political options. However, his ratings in the polls surged to their highest level since the early days of his presidency after he won passage of NAFTA and the Brady Bill. His job approval ratings went up to 58%, higher than Reagan's ratings but lower than Bush's and about the same as Carter's at the end of their first years.

TURNING AROUND THE MARKETING CAMPAIGN

Perhaps the critical turning point for the president was his reaction to the Newt Gingrich-led Republican Party and its proposal to stop lunch programs for the poor and to drastically cut Medicare payments. The president stood up for the underprivileged in this country and fought the Republican leaders in an intense budget battle waged mainly in the media. The battle used all of the trappings that one would find in the best propaganda campaigns that corporate America has waged. In the end, the president refused to give in, and with the support of the American people (polls showed that most Americans agreed with him), the president won the battle and with it their hearts and minds. The result of the battle was the successful reengineering of the president's image to match the mood of the country—right in the center of the political spectrum. The permanent campaign run from the White House since the signing of the budget in October 1995 successfully put Clinton back into the White House and has kept his approval ratings high in the face of allegation after allegation. After the Republicans took over both houses of Congress in 1994, Clinton realized that he had to move back to the centrist position he had veered from during the 2 years since taking office in 1992. In 1995, Clinton decided to turn around his campaign for the hearts and minds of the American people by signing legislation that would balance the budget and effectively end the welfare system as we knew it. As one looks at Clinton's approval ratings from the time of the signing through the 1996 election, he moved consistently upward, culminating with a victory at the polls.

The campaign since the 1995 balance budget signing incorporated policies from both the right and left of the political spectrum. Policies on child care, health care, and education reforms all had liberal dimensions, but at the same time, balancing the budget was accomplished by making government smaller. In effect, the permanent campaign took on a new agenda during this period that brought together both liberal and conservative policies, enabling Clinton to advance new programs and, at the same time, to keep the budget in balance.

The marketing campaign run from the White House during Clinton's second term in office has slowly but surely repositioned the images of both the Democrats and Republicans. By moving the Democrats back to the center of the political spectrum through the various programs and initiatives he has spearheaded, Clinton has successfully repositioned his party so that it appeals to the greatest number of consumers in the marketplace—both liberals and moderates (and even some conservatives). At the same time, Clinton has helped to reposition the image of the Republican Party further to the right on the political spectrum.

The type of image manufacturing that Clinton and his people have engineered is best evidenced by those companies that are able to appeal to segments of all persuasions without cannibalizing anyone in the market. For example, a product such as Coca-Cola appeals to consumers of all ages, making it universally acceptable. Clinton has turned Democratic activism into a form of governing that looks good to a large enough majority of the American people to keep his party in a position of leadership. By casting the Democrats as the party of ideas, Clinton had successfully repositioned his image and the image of the Democratic Party to keep up with the demands of a changing electorate. That image remained intact until the Monica Lewinsky allegations surfaced.

The Impeachment Campaign

There is no doubt that the president ran an effective permanent campaign from the White House if one looks at his job approval ratings from the time the Lewinsky matter was reported in the media until the time he was impeached by the House of the Representatives. The campaign incorporated the use of all the ingredients of a successful election campaign including constant polling, repositioning of the president's image in the public's eye, and a day-to-day strategy that has had the president attending to his business while the Republicans worked at impeaching him.

One of the most potent weapons that the president employed in his latest permanent campaign has been the role played by his wife, Hillary. Similar to the function of opinion leaders in other markets, the first lady has become the president's best advocate, a far cry from her muted role in his 1996 reelection campaign. By deflecting any intrusions into her personal life and standing by her husband, she effectively redirected the debate from the president's poor judgment to the unfair attack on her husband. On the day before the House voted on the impeachment of the president, Hillary Clinton made her strongest personal statement in support of her husband by voicing the pride she has in him. Some even described her as the "Princess Diana" of the Lewinsky scandal, a tragic figure who is beloved by the public.[11]

In turned out that Kenneth Starr, the independent counsel investigating the matter, at times was his own worst enemy. In an interview with a magazine detailing his contacts with reporters, Starr created a serious misimpression that he illegally leaked information. In the interview in *Brill's Content,* a new magazine about the media, the reporter alleges that he has proof that Starr violated the law barring disclosure of grand jury evidence. Steven Brill, the magazine's editor, founder, and author of the story, says that Starr's background briefings for reporters clearly violated the law as interpreted by various courts. In a media release meant to clear up the matter, Starr's office said, "We released information about the circumstances surrounding the initial interview of Ms. Lewinsky but not the substance of the interview." According to Starr, the information amounted to a "limited disclosure" that was "entirely appropriate."[12]

The players in and out of Congress who debated the impeachment process resorted to the parsing of words, hair-splitting, and legalisms in an effort to remanufacture the words and actions of Clinton. In the backs of the minds of the congressional leaders who decided the fate of the president was an attempt to manufacture their own images, ever cognizant of the impact of the shutdowns of the government on their fortunes in the previous two elections.

The trade-off in the public relations campaign that congressional leaders considered was the consequence of acting or not acting on impeachment. Advocates of the president presented the case that they would be lowering the bar for impeaching future presidents if they formally accused Clinton of "high crimes and misdemeanors" for lying about sex and trying to cover it up. On the other side, the accusers of the president made the case that no House of Representatives will ever be able to impeach again because the bar will be so high that only a convicted felon or a traitor could be impeached.

Ultimately, impeachment of the president hinged less on the facts in the case and more on the way in which the Clinton's image was manufactured and presented to the American people and Congress. At the heart of the debate was a very fundamental trade-off, that is, whether Congress and the American people should judge Clinton as a private citizen or as the president of the United States. Some argued that impeachment for high crimes and misdemeanors was meant for the president in his capacity to be a threat to the nation, not for his behavior as a private citizen. Herein lies the two images that Clinton manufactured and promoted as separate and distinct from one another in the minds of many people in this country.

To the extent that Clinton can continue to keep these two images separated in the minds of the American people, his permanent campaign will succeed. However, at the point that these two images converge in people's minds, Clinton's permanent campaign will cease to be effective.

CONCLUSION

One of the best lessons that American marketers have learned in the past decade is that new product development has to be a continuous process. Tom Peters, the management guru, suggests that a company should be producing at least a dozen new ideas each month on how to improve each of its product lines. Everyone in the company is constantly thinking of ways in which to make minor improvements to the product or service. Given the intense competition in most markets today, companies that fail to develop new products expose themselves to great risk. Likewise, the president must be in a position to continually innovate.

Herein lies and accentuates the problems of leadership in a high-tech age. It is not sufficient to pass legislation without an eye toward the impact that the process has on the image of the president as a leader. Successfully using marketing as a governing tool is a much greater challenge than using it as campaign strategy.

Because of the cynicism toward and distrust of Washington, there cannot be a "honeymoon" for a president anymore. It is very hard to do a good job of governing and be political at the same time. Republican strategist William Kristol, quoted in an editorial by David Broder, puts it this way:

> With the political challenges and the decline of the parties, everything is so volatile [that] you need more control in the White House than perhaps you once did. The White House needs to be on top of everything that gets into the evening news. . . . We permitted all kinds of Cabinet fights to go on, and I think we paid a huge price for that down the road.

George Stephanopolous adds,

> First of all, I agree that you do need control in the White House. . . . You cannot separate politics from government at all. There were some stories, even this week, about the endless campaign. There is no way around it. Right now, we have 24-hour news cycles. . . . CNN [en]sures that you are forced to react at any time, and that's going to happen throughout the time of the Clinton presidency. The toughest part of this is discipline. And I think that is going to be the hardest thing we have to grapple with. We have to have discipline, to decide what we want to do to build a consensus to do it and then to stick by it once it's done.[13]

A key issue and problem with Clinton has been his denial of the fact that he does rely on polls to direct his policies and not, as his advisers have insisted, only to track how successful he has been. The fact of the matter is that leadership in the new millennium will depend even more on marketing as it becomes as easy as the push of a button on a computer to stay on top of every utterance the president makes. If Clinton and future presidents are willing to admit to the use of marketing, explain to the American people that they are trying to respond to their needs and wants, and point out that it is being used in a constructive manner, then the political system stands to be strengthened.

Presidents must convince the American people that they have to change their stands on promises they had made not because they are caving in to the interest groups and polls but rather because they are responding to the forces in the political marketplace. This will help the American people to understand the style of leadership that is necessary in the high-tech age in which we live.

Marketing technology has altered the way in which business is conducted in industry after industry, from sports to politics. Herein lies the challenge to the president and to our society in general, and that is the ability to control and manage the use and impact of marketing technology on politics. The critical question that needs to be raised is whether it is even feasible for a president not to be wired in to the public sentiment when his every move is monitored by the media and then broadcast within moments across the information highway. Along with the danger of an overreliance on polls is the wisdom of any good marketer knowing that information is a necessary ingredient to being a successful leader in an age of manufactured images.

NOTES

1. Kotler, P. (1994). *Marketing management* (7th ed.). Englewood Cliffs, NJ: Prentice Hall.

2. Dickson, P. (1994). *Marketing management* (1st ed.). Fort Worth, TX: Dryden.

3. Blumenthal, S. (1980). *The permanent campaign.* New York: Simon & Schuster.

4. Woodward, B. (1994). *The agenda: Inside the Clinton White House.* New York: Simon & Schuster.

5. Baumann, M. (1993, April 28). Poll: Clinton caring, but fails on promises. *USA Today,* p. A2.

6. Gallup Poll. (1993, June 7). The first year favorable poll ratings. *Newsweek,* p. 16.

7. Carney, J. (1994, April 11). Playing the numbers from healthcare to Whitewater, the Clinton administration relies heavily on polling. *Time,* p. 40.

8. See Woodward (Note 4, p. 186).

9. See Woodward (Note 4, pp. 259-260).

10. Jouzaitis, C. (1993, December 26). Clinton's bumpy first year: Failed promises shadow successes. *Chicago Tribune,* sec. 1, pp. 1, 7.

11. Simon, R. (1998, December 19). With "approval and pride," Mrs. Clinton defends her husband. *Chicago Tribune,* sec. 1, p. 1.

12. Associated Press. (1998a, June 16). At age 98, this senior gets high school raves. *Chicago Tribune,* sec. 1, p. 8.

13. Broder, D. (1994, April 6). From the campaign trail, timely words for the White House. *Chicago Tribune,* sec. 1, p. 15.

8

The Solution

The flood of money that gushes into politics today is a pollution of democracy.
—Theodore H. White, author of *The Making of the President 1960,* in *Time,* November 19, 1984

The old way of campaigning is history. Bob Greene, a *Chicago Tribune* columnist, observes that 25 years ago, a campaign manager would expect the candidate to reach perhaps 10,000 people at a big rally in a major city but closer to 50 million people on the evening network news later that night. Consequently, campaign schedules were set up carefully so that a single event a day would be held in time for the evening newscast deadlines. The face-to-face campaign, although interesting, meant very little because it was the big event each day that mattered.

Greene also believes that the lesson of the current campaign finance controversies centers not on whether what was done was legal or illegal but rather on the underlying assumption that more money equals more commercials equals more votes. In other words, a candidate can buy votes by drumming up enough money to air more negative commercials than the opponent and by airing them sooner than the opponent airs his or her commercials. This, he believes, renders the old idea of what a campaign is all but obsolete.[1]

As we continue to see the democratization of countries around the world, the impact of marketing technology on politics will become increasingly more important to control.[2] Just witness the number of countries that have turned to democracy in the past decade. There is a global movement toward democracy taking place that is moving in tandem with technological advances that will subject political systems to pitfalls and challenges never experienced before.

In the future, advances in the telecommunications industry, especially inter-active technology, will have the potential to transform the electoral process as we know it to a more direct democracy. For example, Jill Alper, political director of the Democratic National Committee, announced that as of 1998, every Democratic state party was on-line. In fact, she said that voters in some states are now able to get their absentee ballots over the Internet.[3] Furthermore, in the future, it might be possible for citizens to vote from their own homes on their computers. This change brings with it the potential for substantially increasing the level of participation in presidential elections.

The Internet will continue to shape politics by putting people in closer touch with their government, thus allowing citizens to voice their opinions like never before. In effect, there will be an explosion of microdemocracy. Bob Dole might have been the first political candidate to promote his Web site to build a digital grassroots volunteer network, but he certainly will not be the last. The Web is making political information so easily readable that any individual on-line can research any candidate on any range of issues.

This new digital democracy also will open up the possibility of splinter groups gaining access to the national psyche in a much more direct manner. The Web is beginning to transplant the traditional "mediating institutions," such as political parties and network news journalists, as a primary source of informa-tion. Ultimately, the threat to democracy will be the limits on freedom of speech that might need to be imposed as this medium gains power and familiarity to all Americans. Polling the opinions of people will become even less expensive as the Web becomes more widespread.[4]

The budget battle of late 1995 never would have happened in previous administrations when political parties had tight control over the politicians. In fact, there was almost an unwritten law not to furlough federal workers that was broken during that battle of wills between Bill Clinton and Republican leader Newt Gingrich in 1995.

The gridlock in Washington, D.C., is symbolic of the change that politics has gone through in this country. The political showdowns between the two major parties have become more confrontational and extreme. The shutdown of the government was caused mainly by a minority faction in the Republican Party that pushed for certain measures in the negotiations; some say they did so out of fear of losing their reelection bids. It also happened because a publicly perceived weak president took the opportunity to turn his own political fortunes by taking a tough stand. At the real heart of the shutdown, and one of the serious problems we face in this country, is the increasing number of polls that reveal an electorate fed up with Washington and ready to throw out the incumbent who does not bend to the will of the people.[5]

A NEW AGE IN POLITICS

We are living in a different political era, one where our political leader is supposed to be sensitive and, at the same time, tough. We have accepted our president thinking aloud as he goes on and on debating issues in his own mind. The "new age" president is one who has attended Lamaze classes and family therapy.[6]

Going back to George Washington, presidents always have known that without the public support of the people, they never could enact the policies they thought were good for the people. It turns out that Washington had a terrible temper, one that he worked hard to keep under control. Also, knowing that he was not the most elegant speaker, Washington turned to people such as James Madison and Alexander Hamilton to help him put his ideas into words. In this hi-tech age in which we now live, presidents do not have the luxury of having others speak for them.[7]

Washington Post columnist E. J. Dionne, Jr., has accurately pointed out that one of the significant changes taking place in politics today centers on the movement toward less personal campaigning. In a recent article, Dionne quotes Dan Schnur, former California Governor Pete Wilson's communications director, who comments on the alarming decline of political coverage on television:

> The lack of news coverage itself should be of concern, but it would not be alarming. . . . The preponderance of paid political advertising would be of concern but not alarming. But the combination, the incredible imbalance between paid advertising and news media coverage, is alarming because there is no control [over] the accuracy of the information.[8]

THE EROSION IN PUBLIC CONFIDENCE

Former Senator Paul Simon believes that the public image of Congress is that of an unresponsive institution. In reality, Simon believes that Congress is excessively responsive—to the polls and to campaign contributors. He believes that this responsiveness (to the wrong people) is at the heart of the campaign financing problem in this country, and one that is leading to an erosion of national leadership.[9]

Newton Minow, former chairman of the Federal Communication Commission, has succinctly identified why there is a public erosion in national leadership in the United States today. He believes that people in this country are tired of a presidential nominating system in which a small group of political activists in Iowa and New Hampshire have such a great influence on the nominating process. Minow draws a comparison to Chicago politics, where it requires fewer voters in the whole state of Iowa or New Hampshire to elect someone than it would to carry only 2 of Chicago's 50 municipal wards. He also thinks that people in this country are tired of a system in which candidates continue to use negative commercials that attack their opponents. Minow believes that people are tired of a system that forces candidates to raise the lion's share of their campaign "war chests" from special interest groups to ensure that they will get their parties' nominations months before the national conventions. People also are sick of a system in which millions of Americans are neither Republicans nor Democrats and want nothing to do with the nominating process, Minow believes. More than 40% of the American people identify themselves as independent voters, not participating because they must identify themselves as either Democrats or Republicans to vote. According to Minow, this eliminates the broad center of the political spectrum that should participate. Furthermore, Minow goes on to say that convention delegates have little time to meet and debate the issues before their party platforms are developed.[10]

One of the consequences of the mass marketing of politics is the postelection popularity that comes with running for office in the high-tech age. It is not uncommon to find candidates who lose their bids for national office turning to television as an outlet for the frustration that they might have felt during the course of their long, hard-fought campaigns. For example, in 1994, Dan Quayle turned his spelling fiasco of the word "potato" into a commercial spot for Lay's potato chips. Dole endorsed a $299 round-trip ticket to Paris just days after he lost the 1996 election to Clinton; it should be noted that Dole then donated his $3,000 fee to a community center for the elderly. Former vice presidential candidate Geraldine Ferraro promoted Diet Pepsi, taking advantage of her political fame that ultimately landed her a job on CNN's *Crossfire* program. Former New York Governor Mario Cuomo and former Texas Governor Ann Richards even appeared together in a commercial for Doritos corn chips in a 1995 Super Bowl commercial. It is hard to imagine that these types of activities are building public confidence in our system.[11]

Contributing to the erosion of public confidence in political leaders is the plethora of ethics investigations, not only of the president but also of other influential leaders in Congress. For example, a 2-year ethics committee investigation found that in 1990, the Lincoln Foundation began paying for television broadcasts, ostensibly for educational purposes. But GOPAC, Gingrich's conservative political action organization, identified the broadcasts as an attempt to bring voters into the Republican Party.[12]

The American people have been exposed to the fund-raising tactics of the Democrats in the campaign finance reform hearings. What has not been made as visible, however, are the same tactics on the Republican side. For example, for the more than 200 people who were the most generous contributors to the Republican Party in the 1996 presidential cycle, an exclusive Florida resort was the setting for an evening of food, drinks, and shoulder-rubbing with the Senate majority leader, the House Appropriations Committee chairman, and other lawmakers. An even more distinguished club was called the "Team 100," a group of donors who gave the Republican National Committee $175,000 over a 4-year period and who met with an exclusive group of powerful politicians, all expenses paid, at another resort on the ocean in Palm Beach, Florida. In the past, members of the Team 100 have hob-knobbed with politicians in meetings in Rome, Paris, Vienna, and other European cities. Contributors to the Team 100 paid $100,000 to join the group and $25,000 annually for 3 years of the 4-year membership. Membership in this exclusive club topped 300 during the 1996 presidential election campaign and then dropped by as much as 100 soon after the election.[13]

THE COST OF RUNNING FOR POLITICAL OFFICE

The current campaign finance problem was made worse by a 1976 Supreme Court decision that equated free spending with free speech. By including campaign spending as part of the First Amendment, the Supreme Court made any efforts to reform the system difficult, if not impossible.[14] This means that the richer one is, the more free speech one possesses, whereas those without money are proportionately denied free speech. In practice, this ruling prevents any limitation on campaign advertising. If there is no limit on advertising, then there never will be any limit to the need for money to run a candidate's marketing campaign, making him or her open to the influence of those with money. Unfortunately, the role of money has become so pervasive and influential that it has radically changed the American electoral system, turning political campaigns into full-fledged advertising campaigns.[15]

Concerned with escalating costs of campaigns, Congress passed legislation in 1974 limiting individuals to $1,000 donations per candidate for federal office and capped total contributions for each individual at $25,000 per election. The same legislation allowed individuals to give $20,000 in "hard money" contributions (i.e., money that has to be reported to the Federal Election Commission [FEC]) to political parties to be spent directly on a presidential or congressional campaign and allowed them to give unlimited funds in "soft money" contributions (i.e., money raised outside FEC limits and not spent to promote individual candidates) to parties for general purposes.

The cost to run for office at any level in government is skyrocketing. In 1996, the Dole and Clinton campaigns each received $37 million in primary matching funds and approximately $62 million for the campaigns they waged in the fall. According to Common Cause, from January 1995 through June 1996, more than $75 million was raised by Republican national organizations and more than $65 million was raised by Democratic national organizations in soft money contributions.[16]

The age of the campaign button is leaving political life as we know it very quickly. For example, to get elected alderman in Chicago costs at least $50,000. The cost of 1,000 window signs is $800, yard signs cost 30 cents each, buttons cost about 10 cents each, and 500 videotapes cost $3,000.[17] In 1996, $2.6 billion was spent to elect 476 people to federal office, twice as much as was spent in 1984.[18]

Let us look at the cost of running an organization for a candidate running in a presidential primary. When Phil Gramm ran for the Republican nomination in 1996, he paid the person running his Florida campaign a consulting fee of $7,500 a month. Gramm's field director in Florida, whose responsibility was to court delegates for that primary, was paid $10,000 a month. He also racked up a $500,000 bill trying to court those delegates. In the first three quarters of 1995, Gramm had already spent approximately $13 million in his bid for the nomination. For the first three quarters of 1995, a time when Gramm looked as if he had a good chance of winning the nomination, his campaign aides took in $52,000 a day. At the same time, they were spending $53,000 a day.

Lamar Alexander, another Republican looking for the nomination in 1995, spent $27,500 a month in consulting fees for the services of Mike Murphy, his chief strategist. On top of the monthly outlay, Murphy spent $400,000 on advertising in the third quarter of 1995 alone. California Governor Pete Wilson, also seeking the Republican nomination, was spending $20,000 a month for two of his top advisers, Craig Fuller and George Gorton, and approximately $10,000 a month for each of four different fund-raising consultants. Dole's campaign manager was paid a gross salary of $125,000 a year.[19]

It was estimated that a candidate who ran in 1996 needed at least $44.7 million in private contributions and federal matching funds to make a serious run for the office. In a study conducted on the previous spending in presidential campaigns in both parties since 1976, the candidate who raised the most money in the year preceding the general election went on to win the nomination (excluding John Connally's bid for the Republican nomination in 1980).[20]

Looking back at the 1996 presidential campaign, by Election Day, the Democrats spent $250 million and the Republicans spent $400 million in what was the most expensive presidential campaign in history, nearly twice as expensive as the campaign in 1992. In 1992, the Democrats spent $85 million in hard money and the Republicans spent $164 million. That compares to $146 million spent by the Democrats in hard money and $278 million by the Republicans in 1996. In the soft money category, in 1992, the Democrats raised

$31 million and the Republicans raised $46 million. In this same category in 1996, the Democrats raised $106 million and the Republicans raised $121 million.[21]

In 1996, a record $2.2 billion was spent by the two major political parties, political action committees (PACs), and other groups. During the 1996 campaign, 92% of House races and 88% of Senate races were won by the candidates who spent the most money. Today, the average amount of money spent by a winner in the Senate is $4.6 million; in the House, the average is $673,000. On the other hand, the average amount of money spent by losers in Senate races was $2.7 million and in House races was $265,000. The most expensive campaign in the Senate during the 1996 election was waged by Jesse Helms, who spent approximately $14 million. In the House, Richard Gephardt waged the most expensive campaign, spending $5.5 million. Dole spent the most of any presidential candidate in 1996, with an outlay of $131 million, followed by Clinton ($112 million), Steve Forbes ($42 million), and Pat Buchanan ($32 million). During the 1992 campaign, Clinton spent approximately $40 million in defeating George Bush but spent close to $100 million in advertising alone to beat Dole in 1996. Costs will escalate in campaigns in the future.[22]

So, what is pushing up the cost to run for office? The answer lies in the fact that candidates need money to get the necessary name recognition to manufacture their images in the marketplace. Without a full-blown advertising campaign, it has become nearly impossible to disseminate a candidate's message to the electorate. To successfully craft an image, there must be a large number of repeated exposures in a very short period of time. For example, on "Super Tuesday," when candidates have to get their messages out to several different states on the same day, they literally have no choice but to rely on full-blown advertising campaigns to do the job. Advertising campaigns have become the assembly line that candidates use to manufacture their images. Keep in mind that it is not money alone that ensures victory at the ballot box, but without money, candidates no longer have an opportunity to compete effectively in the current nominating system.[23]

WORKING AROUND THE RULES

Presidential candidates are adept at getting around the "rules of the game." For example, during the 1996 campaign, Dole used a special account set up to defray legal fees as another way in which to pay for salaries and events. In fact, his general election campaign borrowed $1.2 million from this fund.[24] There are other ways in which to get around the current legal system, allowing candidates to circumvent the funding restrictions currently in place. For example, groups can mount their own issue campaigns so long as they stop short of telling people to vote for a specific candidate; donors can give unlimited

amounts of money to build their parties, which often results in running candi-
date-oriented ads; supporters can donate large amounts of money to their parties
but discreetly indicate which candidates should benefit; and foreigners, barred
from contributing money, can donate through residents and American sub-
sidiaries.

There are many examples of how candidates at different levels of government
have gotten around the rules. In 1996, the AFL-CIO spent a record $35 million
on radio, television, and field operations. During the final weeks before the
election, the union paid $8 million to educate voters and, at the same time, to
attack candidates not supportive of their issues. The Christian Coalition distributed 45 million voter guides through 100,000 different churches in the final
week of the campaign. The FEC accused the coalition of working with the
Republican Party and forced the coalition to make its flyers less obviously
partisan.[25]

Just look at the size of the contributions that different organizations made to
both Republicans and Democrats. The following organizations made significant
donations to the Republicans[26]:

Philip Morris	$2,508,118
RJR Nabisco	$1,148,175
American Financial Group	$ 794,000
Joseph E. Seagram & Sons	$ 685,145
Brown & Williamson	$ 635,000
News Corporation	$ 604,700
AT&T	$ 546,440
U.S. Tobacco	$ 539,253

Democrats also fared well. The following organizations made significant
contributions to the Democratic Party:

Communications Workers of America	$1,108,425
American Federation of State, City, and Municipal Employees	$1,069,550
Walt Disney	$ 997,050
Joseph E. Seagram & Sons	$ 945,700
United Food & Commercial Workers	$ 707,550
Revelon Group/MacAndrews & Forbes Holding	$ 648,250
Lazard Freres	$ 617,000
Loral	$ 600,500
MCI Telecommunications	$ 593,603
Laborers International Union of North America	$ 580,400

In future elections, the cost of running for the presidency will go up by a staggering 40% a year, according to Ralph Reed, former executive director and political strategist of the Christian Coalition and now the president of his own political consulting firm. In 1996, candidates who took federal matching funds spent $37 million through the primary season. In the year 2000, this will increase to approximately $50 million, with the cycle continuing to increase by the same percentage every 4 years unless something is done to stop the current spending binge.[27]

THE GROWTH AND FUTURE
OF THIRD PARTIES

Third parties in the United States date back to the early 1900s. In Chicago in 1912, the Progressive Party, led by Teddy Roosevelt, attracted quite a mix of voters including thinkers, social workers, disgruntled Republicans, and businesspersons. The message of Roosevelt's third party was a new nationalism, advocating more progressive immigration laws and voting rights for women. This ultimately split the Republican Party, with 27% shifting to Roosevelt and 23% staying with the Republican Party. The net result was a win for the Democratic candidate, Woodrow Wilson, who amassed just 42% of the vote and won with an electoral college landslide. In 1968, George Wallace, leading the American Independents, attracted 13% of the vote, giving Richard Nixon (43.4%) a slight margin over Hubert Humphrey (42.7%). In 1992, Ross Perot won more than 19% of the voters with his third-party bid by his United We Stand party. This pushed the election into the lap of Clinton over Bush, as Clinton won with 43% of the vote compared to Bush's 37%.[28]

Third parties will continue to flourish in the future if either one of the two major parties becomes too extreme in its views, thus alienating major segments of voters. For example, the former head of the Republican Party, Haley Barbour, warns that the Republican Party needs to win over women voters and minorities if it is going to have a chance of retaking the White House. According to Barbour, in 1996, the Republican Party failed to get the support of many minority and women voters, thus crippling the party's chances of winning the presidency. Barbour also believes that the party needs to combat the perception that it is controlled by the social conservatives, with opposition to abortion as its primary issue of concern.[29]

HAVE THE MEDIA GONE TOO FAR?

The affair between Clinton and White House intern Monica Lewinsky raises a very serious question in this country with respect to whether the media have begun to dig too deeply into the personal lives of our leaders. The problem lies in the extent to which the media have decided to go to get a story out that will attract readers. For example, the *New York Post* quoted a London *Sun* interview with Adam Dave, an ex-boyfriend of Lewinsky who said that, as a teenager, she liked to handcuff him to a bed. Or, consider the *Washington Post* article in which a coworker of Lewinsky was quoted as saying that in 1995, she talked about how she wanted to have sex in the Oval Office and, in particular, on the desk. The questions appropriately raised by Tom Rosenstiel, a *Los Angeles Times* columnist and director of the Project for Excellence in Journalism, are as follows. What must be learned about Lewinsky to evaluate her credibility? Is her sexual history something that is necessary to know to make this evaluation?

A very well-respected journalist, Gloria Borger of *U.S. News & World Report,* was quoted as saying that she is troubled by the anonymous quotes about what a "slut" Lewinsky is. The real issue raised by Mary Matalin, a Republican activist and radio news show host, is whether the people coming out now and talking about Lewinsky are after a book deal or simply publicity. The same issues raised here can include the coverage of Clinton's private life since he entered the White House and what level of coverage is necessary and fair in reporting on the president.

According to Rosenstiel, some newspapers in this country have followed an unwritten rule that a journalist cannot use an anonymous source to impugn a person's reputation. Rosenstiel makes the point that this rule is not much in evidence now. We also have now seen, for the first time, a story that never was published being retracted. On CNN's *Larry King Live,* while interviewing William Ginsburg, Lewinsky's first attorney, Larry King told the lawyer that the next day the *New York Times* was going to report that there is information in a message on Lewinsky's phone-answering machine that would be very revealing of the president's motives. Moments later in the program, King issued a "clarification," admitting that he might have jumped too soon with that statement. Everyone seems to be jumping in the media, not only too soon with stories in general but with stories and information that belong in the tabloids, not in the traditional media.[30]

As we enter the new world of digital communications, it will become difficult for editors to do what *Newsweek* did right before the magazine was about to break the Lewinsky story, which was to apply the standard of skeptical doubt when sources cannot be relied on. *Newsweek,* at the last minute, decided not to let the story break and was beat to the punch by Matt Drudge, founder of the *Drudge Report,* a Web site that disseminates rumors about politicians.

The Internet effectively removes the expertise of editors who do not have an opportunity to screen what is being said. There are market forces at work that will make it increasingly difficult to withhold a story when the thirst for information about a scandal is so strong. But these same market forces will create problems for journalists that will further erode the confidence the public has in the media.

For example, the *Dallas Morning News* posted a story on the Web version of the newspaper that a Secret Service agent was prepared to testify that he witnessed the president in a compromising position with a young woman. However, within hours, the story had to be retracted. The verification that should have gone on before the story was reported was delayed until after the fact, further damaging the president's image in the process. Unfortunately for the president, the retraction was too late to stop the downloading of the story onto several other databases around the world.

In August 1997, a group of publishers, editors, and reporters from newspaper, radio, and television news organizations met at Harvard University to discuss ways in which to deal with their concerns for the industry. The group decided to start a national movement of self-reflection and a renewal of its dedication to the values that drive journalistic practices in the public interest. The group decided to have several forums around the country at which top journalists would be invited to share their thoughts and concerns with interested members of the public and journalism students. The group was formally called the Committee of Concerned Journalists and has issued a call for others to join. One of the most important conclusions drawn from this conference was that the First Amendment implies obligation as well as freedom.

One of the panelists at a forum held at Northwestern University in November 1997 was Jack Fuller, president of the Tribune Publishing Company, who said,

> Journalism has the responsibility to tell the truth so [that] people have the information they need to be sovereign. . . . Journalists are losing trust not because of the purpose they serve but [because of] how we do our work. . . . We give insufficient attention to the harm we cause and fail to value the damage we do, we invade privacy too many times, [and] we reduce news to the least common denominator.[31]

HOW DO WE CHANGE THE SYSTEM?

Something needs to be done to fix our political system. There are several different general courses of action to turn the system around in a positive direction.[32]

1. One approach closely mirrors the McCain-Feingold campaign reform bill, which is to ban all soft money, limit the contributions from PACs, and set voluntary spending limits for political candidates.

2. A second approach would be to amend the Constitution by instituting spending caps, thereby limiting the need for money to be contributed to political candidates. This, however, would violate the right to free speech, according to recent rulings by the Supreme Court.

3. A third approach would center on taxpayer involvement and offer public financing to candidates who agree to spending caps.

4. A fourth approach would be to put the burden on the media's shoulders and offer candidates cheaper airtime in an effort to cut campaign costs.

5. A fifth approach would be to lift all limits on money but to require greater regulations on disclosure of donations.

A result of buying and selling access is that the campaign process has turned into a corrupt process that trivializes public discourse. Minow has his own ideas on how to fix the system. He suggests requiring broadcasters to give free airtime to candidates for public office as a condition of getting access to technology necessary to handle digital programming. Furthermore, as a condition of accepting that offer, the candidate should agree not to buy any more time on this same medium. Minow believes that it is the purchase of airtime that has driven up the expense of campaigns and the resulting abuses that have accompanied the increase. He believes that if the deep-pocketed candidates did not try to outspend their competition, then the current financial spiral would stop. Minow recommends the following guidelines to correct the system[33]:

1. Candidates should turn to communication media other than television such as print advertising, direct mail, and even door-to-door canvassing.

2. These reforms should be extended beyond the VHF/UHF license holders to Internet and subscription/satellite hookups.

3. Complete, detailed, immediate disclosure of every person, company, or group that gives more than $100 should be required, and there should be a ban on all contributions within 30 days of the election. Minow's logic for the ban is that the candidates and press would have time to point a finger at the people who are doing the financing. Finally, he recommends harsh and swift criminal penalties for violators of the law.

Some believe that the best solution is to stem the flow of money into the system. Suggestions include limiting contributions from individuals to permanent residents of the United States, limiting contributions to no more than $100,000 for a calendar year, not allowing contributions from U.S. subsidiaries of a foreign company or from any foreign-owned corporation, and checking donors giving $5,000 or more through computer databases.[34]

Another set of possible solutions includes the following changes[35]:

1. Improve disclosure and enforcement by having campaigns report on contributions as they deposit the money in banks. Today, voters wait months to find out who gives to campaigns. Also, the FEC should be given the power to impose tough penalties on those who break the laws. Unfortunately, it can take years for the FEC to close cases, usually with little more than a slap on the wrist as a penalty.

2. Increase the individual contribution limits to $5,000. Today, the limit is restricted to $1,000 per candidate for each election, a 20-year-old ceiling that should be changed to reflect an increase along with inflation. This change would reduce the dependency of candidates on money coming from the wrong sources. Furthermore, candidates should be required to raise at least half of their funds from their own constituents. At the same time, the contribution limits for PACs could double to $10,000, along with full and immediate disclosure.

3. Ban all soft money because money that comes from these sources is regularly used for the wrong purposes. Soft money is spent directly by advocacy groups to influence the elections of specific candidates, something not allowed under present law. For example, the infamous "Willie Horton" ad run by the Bush campaign in 1988 was financed in this way. Penalties should be hard and swift for soft money steered directly to campaigns.

4. Subject independent groups to the same limits and disclosures as PACs are subjected. In 1996, at least $100 million was spent by independent groups. There currently are no limits or disclosures on fund-raising and spending by these groups.

5. Allow 1 hour of free airtime for every challenger in each election. This would provide a fair chance for all candidates to get their messages across.

Still another set of possible solutions includes changing the rules of elections for political advertising[36]:

1. To further truth in advertising, every television station should require identification of sponsors both before and after a spot airs. Furthermore, a rating system by an independent watchdog group should rate the accuracy of every commercial. Finally, a tally should be made through the course of a campaign, with final statistics on Election Day on how many times a candidate lied to the public.

2. Give each candidate the right to purchase airtime immediately following an opponent's ad to restate the facts as the opponent sees them. Voters need better information, which would include contrasting positions of candidates, with corrections made immediately to any misrepresentations. In addition, candidates should compile their voting records and make them available to voters through the Internet as well as hard copies to go in public libraries.

On March 1, 1997, Clinton called for free television time for candidates. Unfortunately, few people in Washington are willing to pressure broadcasters to go along with Clinton's idea.[37]

Common Cause President Ann McBride called the failed McCain-Feingold campaign reform bill "an antidote for the campaign scandals that have poisoned our democracy and have caused Americans to grow increasingly dissatisfied with their government." This bill would have prohibited most soft money contributions to the national political parties and would have eliminated the ability of independent groups to direct contributions to specific campaigns. The spending limits offered by this bill were based on the belief that, as Feingold puts it, "there is too much money in politics." In 1979, Congress inadvertently tightened the definition of "contribution" from money donated for "any political purpose" to the much narrower one of money donated "for the purpose of influencing any election for federal office." This change in the law made it a crime to raise hard money that goes straight to the candidates ($1,000 or less per donor) and made an exemption of the huge amounts of soft money that get directed to the parties.[38] But the real problem is not the money but rather the marketing campaign that is propelling candidates to raise the money to fund their promotional strategies. Perhaps the reason that the Senate voted down the bill is that senators stood to hurt themselves in future campaigns if they would have supported this bill.

In August 1997, a Gallup poll asked people to identify what they thought were the most pressing problems facing the country. There were approximately 31 different topics, and campaign finance reform was not one of them. Without public pressure in support of reform, there never will be an interest to change the system on the part of the politicians in Washington. Unfortunately, the attitude of the American people is that even with the passage of reforms, politicians will find ways in which to get around the rules.

As of the spring of 1998, the campaign finance legislation crafted by the Republican leadership went down in defeat in the House. Both Democrats and dissident Republicans complained that they were denied a vote on their proposals. Needing a two-thirds majority to pass, the vote against the bill was 334 to 74. It is interesting to note that Gingrich, who at the time had informally announced that he would be running for president in the year 2000, did not vote on the measure.

If the Republican plan would have passed, then the legislation would have curtailed union political activity and banned large, loosely regulated soft money contributions to the two political parties. It also would have allowed local election officials to verify prospective voters' citizenship and permitted PACs and individuals to donate larger sums of money to candidates than is currently allowed under the law. What was missing in the legislation was a stop to the soft money contributions to state parties, which is then normally channeled into congressional campaigns.

However, three smaller bills were put forward, with two passing and one being shot down. The first bill that passed prohibits noncitizens from making donations or expenditures in connection with a federal election. The second bill to pass requires faster disclosure of contributions. Finally, the third bill brought to the floor but failing to pass would have required unions to obtain written consent from members before being able to use their dues for political purposes. If this is the best that our congressional leaders can do, then the time has come for the people of this country to stand up and demand that changes be made.[39]

Is it impossible to change the system? The answer is *no,* and one need only look to corporate America for direction on this front. Companies regularly stretch themselves to reach goals once thought unattainable. For example, Toshiba's new videocassette recorder was produced with the goal of manufacturing it with half the parts in half the time and at half the cost. After putting the team together, the goal was accomplished with a new model that was produced with 60% fewer parts in 1 year (half the time it normally took). The question is as follows: What does it take to reach goals? Jack Welsh of General Electric says that it takes the ability to smell opportunities, put the right people behind them, give these people a budget to work with, and create an atmosphere in which people share ideas. The same strategy can be used to fix the campaign system.[40]

MAKING THE CASE FOR A STRONGER DEMOCRACY

The strength of our democracy lies with the opportunity of all citizens to play a role in the choice of our leaders. Unfortunately, there is a very disturbing trend in our country's voting patterns. Young people between 18 and 25 years of age are so disillusioned with the "system" that many have simply decided not to vote. We all know that legislators in Washington are going to be most concerned with those issues and policies that affect the citizens who vote. This trend does not bode well for the young people in our society. Something needs to be changed in the system to bring the young people back into the fold.

Furthermore, we know that elected officials in Congress will be subject to the influence of special interest groups who have the ability to wage multimillion-dollar campaigns and seriously influence election outcomes through their soft money contributions. In one of the more significant technological changes that has affected Congress, an electronic screen in the front of the House of Representatives records every legislator's vote anytime a roll call is taken. This is made possible with the push of a button on the seat in front of every congressperson and takes only 15 minutes. Before this technology existed, it took nearly 45 minutes to take a roll call on a vote, thereby inhibiting the use of that tactic and making the legislators' voting records more private. This technology became evident to anyone who watched the tallying of votes on television the day the president was impeached. Interest groups are fully aware of this new technology and use their influence to get roll calls on pending legislation important to them.

Our leaders must have the freedom to communicate with the electorate in the best way possible when they are campaigning and after taking the oath of office. To limit the freedom of speech of anyone, especially political leaders, would destroy the very fabric of the Constitution on which our country is based. However, when it becomes possible for people and organizations to influence public opinion in an unfair manner and to reengineer images of our political leaders that are misleading, then changes that protect the American people need to be made.

The use of marketing by various publics in society is influencing democracy for better and for worse; therefore, it must be studied in view of the powerful position it holds. Marketing is like any other technological advancement from the telegraph, to television, to the computer, each of which has moved political discourse to new heights. However, along with the influence and power of this technology comes a responsibility shared by government, business, the media, and other interested parties that play a role in our political process. Because that responsibility is undefined, the time has come for those using political marketing to accept the fact that it is here to stay and should be used with discretion.

Several solutions have been suggested to put a lid on the increasing amount of money being spent to influence political campaigns and governance. Campaign finance reform must be taken out of the hands of politicians and placed in the hands of a bipartisan commission, a group of professionals without any stake in the laws that affect politicians. To incumbent politicians in Congress or the White House, it would be foolhardy to change laws that would come back to haunt them in the next election. Asking politicians to change the laws is like asking criminals at their own hearings to decide their sentences. Each has a vested interest in the outcome and will not decide with the best interests of society in mind. Hence, a Congress and White House that truly want to fix the system must work together to put the power into the hands of people who have no ax to grind.

The argument put forth in this book rests with my strong conviction that politics today is run like a business, with marketing at the heart of the system, without which any serious candidate or incumbent politician will fail. To fix the system, we must begin not with the symptoms but rather with the real problem, which is the amount of money and time that must be devoted to fuel marketing campaigns. Limits and reforms must begin with the marketing campaign if we are to seriously limit the amounts of money spent in future elections. Because of the wide name recognition and the ability to manufacture and reengineer their images, incumbents currently have a huge advantage in every election cycle. The playing field must be leveled out to ensure that we do not get caught in a battle between the Washington "insiders" and Washington "outsiders." That is not unless a candidate is a millionaire and is willing to spend his or her own money to get elected.

As the technological revolution of the telecommunications industry continues, it becomes much more economically feasible for a politician to talk to one voter or citizen at a time. The possibility of doing this on a targeted basis will increase as the number of people using the Internet expands. The ability to talk directly to the American people is moving in tandem with the great strides made by corporations advertising this way.

Without limiting the free speech of politicians during the course of a campaign, we need to limit the length of time that a candidate can run his or her marketing campaign. This would be similar to the political system in the United Kingdom, where there is a fixed period during which candidates are allowed by law to advertise. In addition to limiting the length of time, corporations that own the television airwaves should free up space on their networks to give candidates and politicians an opportunity to communicate with the American people without having to rely on the contributions of others to pay for it.

Take Latin American countries, for example, where campaigns often have a set time frame. In Paraguay, television commercials can air no more than 120 days before Election Day. Furthermore, campaigns in Paraguay are required to end 2 days before voters go to the polling booths to give them a chance to reflect on the candidates without the influence of last-minute advertising blitzes. Also, Election Day always is on a Sunday to ensure that work does not keep voters from going to the polling booths. One more thing: The bars close down the night before the election and stay closed the next day.

The most alarming statistic cited is this book is that the candidate who spends the most money usually wins an election. That statistic needs to be changed given that any smart politician with the financial means or ability to raise millions will pursue this. The serious question is whether we can, within the constraints of our Constitution, limit the amount of money being spent.

We certainly can pass laws for greater disclosure, a quicker response to candidates who violate the laws, and a limited time during which a candidate can advertise. Soft money contributions must be limited severely or even outlawed to eliminate advertising for a candidate under the guise of advocating a certain issue. In place of soft money contributions should come increased levels of contributions by individuals from $1,000 per candidate to as much as $25,000 per candidate. This would eliminate the influence of interest groups and would spread the influence of individuals.

We need an independent body to oversee political campaigns. This independent body, almost a watchdog group similar to Ralph Nader's on the commercial side, could be publicly financed by allowing individuals to donate money on their tax returns to finance the funding of it. The people who would sit on this body should include representatives from each of the major parties (at all levels of office), third parties who can demonstrate a national presence (e.g., getting at least 10% of the popular vote in an election), media representatives, and representatives from the consulting industry from each of the major parties. This must truly be a bipartisan effort to be effective.

Once this body is enacted, it should have powers that would enable its members to act on activities that are illegal in a timely fashion, unlike the current system in which we have to wait until an election is over before slapping offenders' wrists. This body is necessary as we witness the information highway enabling candidates and politicians to go directly to the citizens of this country without the aid and influence of traditional screening bodies—political parties and the media—to act as referees.

Furthermore, so long as political communication equates with freedom of speech, there never will be a way in which to limit the amount of money that is spent on political advertising campaigns. Therefore, the length of political campaigns must be shortened.

In the commercial marketplace, there are laws that prohibit companies from advertising deceptively. In fact, there are three main categories of deception. One area covers the advertiser who states a mistruth, commonly known as a lie. Another is the advertiser who makes an exaggerated claim. The classic case in this area was Kool-Aid promoting itself as a natural fruit drink when in fact it contained artificial ingredients. The third area deals with the advertiser who leaves a false impression in the minds of the consumers. A classic case here was a Campbell Soup advertisement for its chunky beef soup with a lumberjack sitting down to a bowl of soup and piercing a meat chunk with such a small fork that the meat looked huge to the viewers. We need similar laws in politics. The average American citizen would be shocked to know that the Federal Trade Commission, a body that oversees what corporations say in their commercials and advertisements, has no jurisdiction over what is said in a political commercial.

It has only been during the most recent presidential campaigns that television stations and magazines began to publish what they called "reality checks." In so doing, the media took the literal facts stated in commercial, investigated them, and reported any instances in which the candidates lied. But the penalty to a candidate for lying was only a public slap on the wrist. The bigger problem with these situations, even in the case where a candidate violates a campaign finance law, is that the candidate might have already won office before the case is brought up.

Yes, candidates can say anything they want in a political commercial and not be held liable. The only course of action is for an opponent to retaliate by advertising his or her own version of the truth, starting the back-and-forth advertising wars that only increase the spiraling costs of campaigns. Again, a call is made for a bipartisan panel of experts to form a new independent body to oversee that candidates are held accountable for what is said in political commercials. If candidates knew that they could be held accountable, then they would be careful not to falsely accuse their opponents, putting a limit on the negative advertising that costs so much in dollars and integrity to the system.

Finally, one last problem deals with the mass marketing of politicians and their ideas once they get into office. Politicians at all office levels have their own staffs of pollsters and strategists (or, at a minimum, persons in charge of these activities) who are conducting marketing research in an effort to find the "hot" buttons that will move public opinion in their direction.

Yes, the commodity in the political marketplace is public opinion, and the leader who is able to move public opinion in a desired direction will be successful at putting indirect pressure on legislatures at all levels to push for policies that he or she advocates. With the technological revolution taking place, this process becomes much more focused and targeted at all levels, not just for politicians but also for PACs, talk show radio hosts, and interest groups working to influence public opinion. Not a day goes by without a talk show host spitting out radical views and asking listeners to fax their congresspersons about issues of importance to them. From faxes, we are moving to the use of the Internet and e-mail to send thousands and thousands of messages. Similar to the direct mail industry that sells lists of names, phone numbers, and addresses will be the Internet services that sell the technology that enables people to push a few buttons to hit tens of thousands of people who subscribe to an Internet provider or who are "hotlinked" (i.e., set up to receive e-mail automatically) to a Web site.

An education campaign must be started to make the American people aware of the role that marketing is playing in politics and to know that marketing is here to stay and must be treated in the same way as it is dealt with in the commercial marketplace. There always will be both good and bad uses of marketing technology and people who knowingly abuse it. But we live in a democratic society where everyone has the same access to this technology, and for those with deep pockets, the best and the brightest minds in the political marketing industry can be bought.

However, let it be said that there is nothing as fickle as public opinion—the currency in this marketplace—and for those who think that they have mastered the ability to manipulate public opinion, let them beware. The American people are smart consumers. Citizens must proceed in the political marketplace as they do in the commercial marketplace, with a healthy skepticism and a warning:

Caveat Emptor
(Let the Buyer Beware)

NOTES

1. Green, B. (1997, October 26). The campaign we're not supposed to see. *Chicago Tribune,* sec. 1, p. 2.

2. For a further discussion of the impact of marketing on democracies around the world, see O'Shaughnessy, N. (1990). *The phenomenon of political marketing.* Basingstoke, UK: Macmillan; Harris, P. (Ed.). (1996). Political marketing [special issue]. *European Journal of Marketing, 30*(10/11); and Newman, B. I. (1999). *Handbook of political marketing.* Thousand Oaks, CA: Sage.

3. *C-SPAN* (1998, April 25).

4. Fineman, H. (1997, January 27). Who needs Washington? *Newsweek,* pp. 50-52.

5. Neikirk, W. (1996d, January 7). '90s politics relies on confrontation, not compromise. *Chicago Tribune,* sec. 1, p. 3.

6. Fineman, H. (1993, January 25). The new age president. *Newsweek,* pp. 22-23.

7. Perry, J. (1997, January 20). Under the microscope. *Wall Street Journal,* pp. R7, R9.

8. Dionne, E. J., Jr. (1998a, May 20). Name that candidate: California television takes a pass on covering the real news. *Chicago Tribune,* sec. 1, p. 15.

9. Simon, P. (1995, November 26). Mr. Simon returns from Washington. *Chicago Tribune,* sec. 2, pp. 1, 9.

10. Minow, N. (1995, May 10). A call for taking us back to the way it was. *Chicago Tribune,* sec. 1, p. 25.

11. Anderson, L. (1997, January 3). Sales representatives (and senators and mayors and . . .). *Chicago Tribune,* sec. 5, pp. 1, 4.

12. Page, C. (1996, December 29). GOP, Democrats both guilty of bending campaign money rules too far. *Chicago Tribune,* sec. 1, p. 19.

13. Associated Press. (1997, February 13). Top GOP donors, officials to meet. *Chicago Tribune,* sec. 1, p. 20.

14. Campaign finance can be reformed. (1997, March 3). *Business Week,* p. 122.

15. Pfaff, W. (1997, March 8). Broadcasters should give free time to candidates. *Chicago Tribune,* sec. 1, p. 13.

16. CNN-Time. (1997, November 6). *In focus: Campaign reform.* Available on Internet: http://www.allpolitics.com.

17. Davis, R. (1995, February 26). Campaign buttons may soon bow out. *Chicago Tribune,* sec. 2, pp. 1, 4.

18. Gleckman, H. (1997, March 3). Four simple ways to clean up campaign finance. *Business Week,* pp. 36-38.

19. Harwood, J. (1995, November 20). The Gramm campaign shows where funds go in presidential bids. *Wall Street Journal,* pp. A1, A5.

20. Tackett, M. (1995b, February 23). '96 money game: More early primaries put premium on big political war chests. *Chicago Tribune,* sec. 1, p. 14.

21. Duffy, M., & Gibbs, N. (1996, November 11). Money and politics. *Time,* pp. 33-36.

22. Warren, J. (1997, December 3). The campaign merry-go-round requires ever-deeper pockets. *Chicago Tribune,* sec. 1, pp. 1, 28.

23. For a thorough review of campaign finance reform issues, see Gould, J. (1999). You can't teach a dead dog new tricks: The problem of campaign finance and why reform

has not worked. In B. I. Newman (Ed.), *Handbook of political marketing*. Thousand Oaks, CA: Sage.

24. Associated Press. (1996a, June 22). Fund assists Dole's campaign finances. *Chicago Tribune,* sec. 1, p. 18.

25. Birnbaum, J. H. (1996, October 21). Beating the system. *Time,* pp. 33-38.

26. Burns, A., & Regan, M. B. (1997, March 31). The backlash against soft money. *Business Week,* pp. 33-35.

27. Jackson, D. (1997, December 5). Ralph Reed sees GOP campaign for 2000 presidency as costly, crowded. *Chicago Tribune,* sec. 1, p. 4.

28. Madigan, C. H. (1995, September 27). Third parties legacy: Colorful losers. *Chicago Tribune,* sec. 1, pp. 1, 22.

29. Tackett, M. (1997, January 17). Outgoing GOP chief issues warning. *Chicago Tribune,* sec. 1, p. 3.

30. Kurtz, H. (1998, January 29). Too much background: Special report—Clinton accused. *Washington Post,* p. D1.

31. Kovach, B. (1998, February 1). The brewing backlash. *Chicago Tribune* (Perspective), pp. 1, 4.

32. Gibbs, N., & Duffy, M. (1997, March 17). Legal tender. *Time,* pp. 18-23.

33. McCarron, J. (1997, April 21). This political message was brought to you by . . . *Chicago Tribune,* sec. 1, p. 13.

34. Frisby, M., & Harwood, J. (1997, January 22). Democrats and Clinton, in surprise move, curb contributions, bow to refuse aliens' donations. *Wall Street Journal,* p. A16.

35. Gleckman, H. (1997, March 3). Four simple ways to clean up campaign finance. *Business Week,* pp. 36-38.

36. Buerger, H., & Buerger, T. (1996, Fall). Reform campaigns and candidates, not just campaign finance. *Center House Bulletin,* pp. 7-8.

37. Barrett, A. (1997, March 4). Politics shouldn't rule the airways. *Business Week,* p. 38.

38. Gibbs and Duffy (Note 32).

39. Associated Press. (1998b, March 31). Campaign-funding bills defeated in House vote. *Chicago Tribune,* sec. 1, p. 4.

40. Martin, T. J. (1995, May 29). Jack Welch lets fly on budgets, bonuses, and buddy boards. *Fortune,* pp. 145-146.

Afterword

At the time this book went into production in the summer of 1998, the country still was awaiting a public statement by President Bill Clinton on his alleged affair with Monica Lewinsky. As of December 1998, the November elections have just ended, Newt Gingrich has decided to step down from his post as speaker of the House of Representatives, and Clinton has become the second president in the history of the United States to be impeached.

In one of the more colorful campaigns in the November elections, former professional wrestler Jesse Ventura was elected governor of Minnesota. During Ventura's campaign, one ad depicted two boys playing with an action figure that had a shaved head and bulging muscles ripping through the seams of a dark suit. One of the boys in the commercial was then seen banging the doll's fist on a desk and railing against "Evil Special Interest Man." According to Ventura himself, the doll was the novel item of the campaign and people seemed to enjoy it, so if the doll was marketable, then that was all the better. The doll was expected to be out on the market soon after the election, selling for between $19 and $24, with the proceeds to be split between charity and future campaigns by the new governor.

The public relations battle between the White House and independent counsel Kenneth Starr continued to rage on from June to December 1998. It is clear that Clinton won in the court of public opinion but lost in the court of the House of Representatives. The 6-week period between the end of the November elections and the decision by the House to impeach the president on two articles of impeachment startled even the most seasoned observers of politics.

Instant interactive communication between actors on the political stage and the American people has put our political system into a whirlwind that makes it nearly impossible for anyone to take a minute to sit back and think about what

145

is happening. It is almost as if our political system has gone onto "autopilot," with decisions about elected officials happening at lightning speed, perhaps more out of emotion than out of reason.

The net result of the impeachment of the president is a reflection of the ugly state of affairs in which we find ourselves today. People clearly are divided over the president's actions, and it will be some time before the verdict is in on how well Starr manufactured both his own image and the president's image in his attempt to shape public opinion.

It is clear that government by public opinion is a very dangerous tool on which to rely. With the Democrats victorious in the November elections and the opinion polls indicating that a majority of the American people did not want to see the president impeached, Clinton thought that he was assured of a pass on impeachment. As a result, there was not any talk by the president or his people about a censure resolution. In the days immediately preceding the impeachment vote, the president would have given anything for a censure, but it was too late. In the end, the image of Clinton manufactured by the Republicans on the House Judiciary Committee was far more effective than the remanufacturing process attempted by the president and his fellow Democrats.

At the heart of the final 6 months of 1998, and more pertinent to the thesis of this book, is the fact that politicians in the most recent political campaigns continued to be mass marketed, and the country still faced the unsettling problem of having to rely on manufactured images as the basis for making up their minds.

References

AARP Voter. (1996, Fall). [whole issue].

Anderson, L. (1997, January 3). Sales representatives (and senators and mayors and . . .). *Chicago Tribune,* sec. 5, pp. 1, 4.

Assael, H. (1984). *Consumer behavior and marketing action.* Boston: Kent.

Associated Press. (1994, April 6). At town hall gathering, Clinton defends integrity. *Chicago Tribune,* sec. 1, p. 10.

Associated Press. (1995a, April 18). Gap between rich, poor greatest in U.S., studies find. *Chicago Tribune,* sec. 1, p. 13.

Associated Press. (1995b, January 6). New Internet link lets world watch Congress. *Chicago Tribune,* sec. 1, p. 11.

Associated Press. (1996a, June 22). Fund assists Dole's campaign finances. *Chicago Tribune,* sec. 1, p. 18.

Associated Press. (1996b, April 22). Most Blacks say American Dream impossible to achieve, poll finds. *Chicago Tribune,* sec. 1, p. 1.

Associated Press. (1997, February 13). Top GOP donors, officials to meet. *Chicago Tribune,* sec. 1, p. 20.

Associated Press. (1998a, June 16). At age 98, this senior gets high school raves. *Chicago Tribune,* sec. 1, p. 8.

Associated Press. (1998b, March 31). Campaign-funding bills defeated in House vote. *Chicago Tribune,* sec. 1, p. 4.

Barrett, A. (1997, March 4). Politics shouldn't rule the airways. *Business Week,* p. 38.

Baumann, M. (1993, April 28). Poll: Clinton caring, but fails on promises. *USA Today,* p. A2.

Begley, A. (1995, October 8). Serious play [book review]. *Chicago Tribune,* sec. 14, pp. 1-2.

Beher, R. (1997, February 3). Who's reading your e-mail? *Fortune,* pp. 57-70

Bigness, J. (1998, January 30). Clinton's crisis, Internet's boom. *Chicago Tribune,* sec. 2, p. 1.

147

Birnbaum, J. H. (1996, October 21). Beating the system. *Time,* pp. 33-38.

Block, R. (1998, February 9). Congo's name is new, but one face looks a bit familiar. *Wall Street Journal,* pp. A1, A10.

Blumenthal, S. (1980). *The permanent campaign.* New York: Simon & Schuster.

Booz, Allen & Hamilton. (1982). *New products management for the 1980's.* New York: Author.

Broder, D. (1994, February 23). Who will sort out true from false if the media can't? *Chicago Tribune,* sec. 1, p. 19.

Broder, D. (1994, April 6). From the campaign trail, timely words for the White House. *Chicago Tribune,* sec. 1, p. 15.

Browning, G. (1997, June/July). Updating electronic democracy. *Database,* p. 53.

Bruck, C. (1994, May 30). Hillary the pol. *The New Yorker,* p. 58.

Buerger, H., & Buerger, T. (1996, Fall). Reform campaigns and candidates, not just campaign finance. *Center House Bulletin,* pp. 7-8.

Burns, A., & Regan, M. B. (1997, March 31). The backlash against soft money. *Business Week,* pp. 33-35.

Campaign finance can be reformed. (1997, March 3). *Business Week,* p. 122.

Carlson, M., Painton, P., & Kramer, M. (1993, May 31). Shear dismay. *Time,* pp. 20-23.

Carney, J. (1994, April 11). Playing the numbers from healthcare to Whitewater, the Clinton administration relies heavily on polling. *Time,* p. 40.

Chapman, S. (1995, May 7). Sneak attack. *Chicago Tribune,* sec. 4, p. 3.

Cloud, J. (1998, November 16). Give'em hell Hillary. *Time,* p. 52.

CNN-Time. (1997, November 6). *In focus: Campaign reform.* Available on Internet: http://www.allpolitics.com.

Coates, J. (1995a, April 2). Finding poetry in the Net. *Chicago Tribune,* sec. 7, pp. 1, 4.

Coates, J. (1995b, April 3). Untangling the Web. *Chicago Tribune,* sec. 3, p. 1.

Coates, J. (1998, January 22). Internet gossip monger makes front page splash. *Chicago Tribune,* sec. 1, p. 13.

Cochran, W. (1996, April). The boys on the Net. *American Journalism Review,* pp. 40-42.

Cortese, A., & Verity, J. (1995, February 27). Cyberspace. *Business Week,* pp. 78-86.

C-SPAN (1998, April 25).

Davis, R. (1995, February 26). Campaign buttons may soon bow out. *Chicago Tribune,* sec. 2, pp. 1, 4.

Dellios, H. (1994, June 21). Unflappable prosecutor may face no-win situation. *Chicago Tribune,* sec. 1, p. 15.

Democracy and technology. (1995, June 17). *The Economist,* pp. 21-23.

Dickson, P. (1994). *Marketing management* (1st ed.). Fort Worth, TX: Dryden.

Dionne, E. J., Jr. (1998a, May 20). Name that candidate: California television takes a pass on covering the real news. *Chicago Tribune,* sec. 1, p. 15.

Dionne, E. J., Jr. (1998b, April 29). Reinventing government so that it's useful. *Chicago Tribune,* sec. 1, p. 19.

Dowd, M. (1996, May 20). Dole's bid to seem down-home needs a dose of theatrics. *Chicago Tribune,* sec. 1, p. 15.

Drew, B. (1995, October 15). Dream interpretation [book review]. *Chicago Tribune,* sec. 14, p. 5.

Duffy, M., & Gibbs, N. (1996, November 11). Money and politics. *Time,* pp. 33-36.

Etzioni, A. (1995, September 13). The politics of morality. *Wall Street Journal,* p. A14.

Fineman, H. (1993, January 25). The new age president. *Newsweek,* pp. 22-23.

Fineman, H. (1997, January 27). Who needs Washington? *Newsweek,* pp. 50-52.

Friedman, T. L. (1992, November 12). Clinton to open military's ranks to homosexuals. *New York Times,* pp. A1, A9.

Frisby, M., & Harwood, J. (1997, January 22). Democrats and Clinton, in surprise move, curb contributions, bow to refuse aliens' donations. *Wall Street Journal,* p. A16.

Gallup Poll. (1993, June 7). The first year favorable poll ratings. *Newsweek,* p. 16.

Gibbs, N., & Duffy, M. (1997, March 17). Legal tender. *Time,* pp. 18-23.

Gleckman, H. (1997, March 3). Four simple ways to clean up campaign finance. *Business Week,* pp. 36-38.

Goff, L. (1996, September 2). The Webbing of the president. *ComputerWorld,* pp. 79-80.

Goldman, P., DeFrank, T. M., Miller, M., Murr A., & Mathews, T. (1994). *Quest for the presidency 1992.* College Station: Texas A & M Press.

Gould, J. (1999). You can't teach a dead dog new tricks: The problem of campaign finance and why reform has not worked. In B. I. Newman (Ed.), *Handbook of political marketing.* Thousand Oaks, CA: Sage.

Gray, P. (1998, November 16). Body slam. *Time,* p. 57.

Green, B. (1997, October 26). The campaign we're not supposed to see. *Chicago Tribune,* sec. 1, p. 2.

Griffin, J. L. (1995, May 4). More campaigns spinning a political Web. *Chicago Tribune,* sec. 2, pp. 1, 4.

Grigsby, J. (1996, Fall). Catching up to political ads. *Public Relations Quarterly, 41,* 31-33.

Grumman, C. (1996, October 8). Dole error hurts Web site plug. *Chicago Tribune,* sec. 1, p. 19.

Guernsey, L. (1996, May 3). The electronic soapbox. *Chronicle of Higher Education,* p. A29.

Hardy, T. H., & Madigan, C. (1996, August 16). Dole to America: You can trust me. *Chicago Tribune,* sec. 1, pp. 1, 22.

Harris, P. (Ed.). (1996). Political marketing [special issue]. *European Journal of Marketing, 30*(10/11).

Harwood, J. (1995, November 20). The Gramm campaign shows where funds go in presidential bids. *Wall Street Journal,* pp. A1, A5.

Haynes, D. V. (1996, October 25). King speech in GOP ad sparks furor. *Chicago Tribune,* sec. 1, p. 10.

Haynes, D. (1997, March 9). Alliance responds to Christian right. *Chicago Tribune,* sec. 1, p. 4.

Ingalls, Z. (1993, April 28). Oklahoma archive of 50,000 radio and television commercials for political campaigns. *Chronicle of Higher Education,* sec. B4, p. 1.

Institute of Politics. (1981). *Campaign for president: The managers look at '80.* Cambridge, MA: Harvard University, John F. Kennedy School of Government, Institute of Politics.

Institute of Politics. (1985). *Campaign for president: The managers look at '84.* Cambridge, MA: Harvard University, John F. Kennedy School of Government, Institute of Politics.

Institute of Politics. (1989). *Campaign for president: The managers look at '88.* Cambridge, MA: Harvard University, John F. Kennedy School of Government, Institute of Politics.

Jackson, D. (1997, December 5). Ralph Reed sees GOP campaign for 2000 presidency as costly, crowded. *Chicago Tribune,* sec. 1, p. 4.

Jacoby, M. (1996a, September 14). Christian Coalition rally bashes Democrats. *Chicago Tribune,* sec. 1, p. 3.

Jacoby, M. (1996b, September 13). Signs hint Christian Coalition influence has peaked. *Chicago Tribune,* sec. 1, pp. 1, 24.

Johnson, D. W. (in press). *No place for amateurs: The professionalization of modern campaigns.* London: Routledge.

Jones, P. M. (1998, May 31). Competition fuels colleges' megabucks fundraising. *Chicago Tribune,* sec. 1, p. 1.

Jones, T. (1996, May 5). Conventional challenge. *Chicago Tribune,* sec. 1, pp. 1-2.

Jouzaitis, C. (1993, December 26). Clinton's bumpy first year: Failed promises shadow successes. *Chicago Tribune,* sec. 1, pp. 1, 7.

Kirk, J. (1998, June 19). Tax-and-spend theme of ad blitz arrarently hit home with senators. *Chicago Tribune,* sec. 1, p. 3.

Klotz, R. (1997). Positive spin: Senate campaigning on the Web. *Political Science & Politics, 30,* 482-486.

Kotler, P. (1994). *Marketing management* (7th ed.). Englewood Cliffs, NJ: Prentice Hall.

Kovach, B. (1998, February 1). The brewing backlash. *Chicago Tribune* (Perspective), pp. 1, 4.

Krauthammer, C. (1995a, January 6). GOP's agenda should include restoring presidential powers. *Chicago Tribune,* sec. 1, p. 23.

Krauthammer, C. (1995b, February 24). In his presidential bid, Dole can capitalize on JFK. *Chicago Tribune,* sec. 1, p. 15.

Krauthammer, C. (1996, October 28). And that's the truth—Sort of. *Chicago Tribune,* sec. 1, p. 15.

Kurtz, H. (1998, January 29). Too much background: Special report—Clinton accused. *Washington Post,* p. D1.

Lacayo, R. (1998, March 16). All the president's movies: Musclehead or sex fiend—The image of the chief executive is no longer a winning ticket. *Time,* pp. 72-73.

Landler, M. (1992, July 6). How good are polls? We refuse to answer. *Business Week,* pp. 29-30.

Lichtman, A. J., & DeCell, K. (1990). *The 13 keys to the presidency.* Lanham, MD: Madison Books.

Locin, M. (1995, December 26). Cyber chant: Whole world is interacting. *Chicago Tribune,* sec. 2, pp. 1-2.

Longworth, R. C. (1966, April 28). The dream, in pieces: America's economic woes are becoming a crisis of spirit. *Chicago Tribune,* sec. 2, pp. 15-20.

Madigan, C. H. (1995, September 27). Third parties legacy: Colorful losers. *Chicago Tribune,* sec. 1, pp. 1, 22.

Madigan, C. (1996, August 15). Dole at last wears GOP mantle: Candidate called man of honor. *Chicago Tribune,* sec. 1, pp. 1, 26.

Malanowski, J. (1997, August 4). The celluloid senator. *Time,* p. 18.

Martin, T. J. (1995, May 29). Jack Welch lets fly on budgets, bonuses, and buddy boards. *Fortune,* pp. 145-146.

McCarron, J. (1997, April 21). This political message was brought to your by . . . *Chicago Tribune,* sec. 1, p. 13.

McDonald, K. (1996, January 5). Scholarship. *Chronicle of Higher Education,* pp. A7-A14.

McGeary, J. (1996, December 16). Mix and match. *Time,* pp. 29-33.

McGinniss, J. (1968). *The Selling of the president.* New York: Trident.

Miller, A. H., & Gronbeck, B. E. (Eds.). (1994). *Presidential campaigns and American self-images.* Boulder, CO: Westview.

Miller, L. (1996, October 9). Oh, what a tangled Web of studies. *USA Today,* pp. D1-D2.

Minow, N. (1995, May 10). A call for taking us back to the way it was. *Chicago Tribune,* sec. 1, p. 25.

Money and politics: Politicians for rent. (1997, February 8). *The Economist,* pp. 23-25.

Morris, D. (1997). *Behind the Oval Office: Winning the presidency in the nineties.* New York: Random House.

Mosley, R. (1997, March 18). British race to have an American accent. *Chicago Tribune,* sec. 1, p. 3.

Neikirk, W. (1994, April 9). Selling health plan: Clinton '94 campaign. *Chicago Tribune,* sec. 1, pp. 1, 10.

Neikerk, W. (1996a, May 26). Campaigns breed elements of character and caricatures. *Chicago Tribune,* sec. 1, p. 6.

Neikirk, W. (1996b October 25). Clinton's message with a twang. *Chicago Tribune,* sec. 1, p. 16.

Neikirk, W. (1996c, August 20). Crash's reminder: President never travels alone. *Chicago Tribune,* sec. 1, p. 3.

Neikirk, W. (1996d, January 7). '90s politics relies on confrontation, not compromise. *Chicago Tribune,* sec. 1, p. 3.

Neikirk, W. (1997a, January 20). Bully pulpit renews its power. *Chicago Tribune,* sec. 1, pp. 1, 13.

Neikirk, W. (1997b, January 26). Celebrity in chief: Reverence or fodder for the soaps? *Chicago Tribune,* sec. 2, pp. 1, 13.

Newman, B. I. (1988). A services oriented strategic framework for politicians. In *Proceedings of the seventeenth annual Decision Science Institute Western Regional Conference* (pp. 192-195). Honolulu, HI: Decision Science Institute.

Newman, B. I. (1993, June). The role of marketing in the 1992 U.S. presidential election: How Bill Clinton was transformed from "Slick Willie" to "Mr. President." *Werbeforschung & Praxis,* pp. 195-201.

Newman, B. I. (1994). *The marketing of the president: Political marketing as campaign strategy.* Thousand Oaks, CA: Sage.

Newman, B. I. (1999). *Handbook of political marketing.* Thousand Oaks, CA: Sage.

Noble, P. (1996, July). Net the vote. *Campaigns & Elections,* pp. 27-31.

O'Shaughnessy, N. (1990). *The phenomenon of political marketing.* Basingstoke, UK: Macmillan.

Page, C. (1996, December 29). GOP, Democrats both guilty of bending campaign money rules too far. *Chicago Tribune,* sec. 1, p. 19.

Parasuraman, A., Zeithaml, V. A., & Berry, L. L. (1985). A conceptual model of service quality and its implications for future research. *Journal of Marketing, 44.*

Perloff, R. (1997). *Political communication: Politics, press, and public in America.* Hillsdale, NJ: Lawrence Erlbaum.

Perry, J. M. (1994, January 10). Young guns: A second generation of political handlers outduels forebears. *Wall Street Journal,* pp. A1, A7.

Perry, J. (1997, January 20). Under the microscope. *Wall Street Journal,* pp. R7, R9.

Peters, T. (1994, September 5). Asking me is not a solution: Do something. *Chicago Tribune,* sec. 4, p. 3.

Peterson, R., Balasubramanian, S., & Bronnenberg, B. J. (1997). Exploring the implications of the Internet for consumer marketing. *Journal of the Academy of Marketing Science, 4,* 329-346.

Pfaff, W. (1997, March 8). Broadcasters should give free time to candidates. *Chicago Tribune,* sec. 1, p. 13.

Phillips, J. (n.d.). *The age of the infotoxin.* Available on Internet: http://www.adbusters.org/adbusters/.

Pika, J. A., Mosley, Z., & Watson, R. A. (1992). *The presidential contest: With a guide to the 1992 presidential race.* Washington, DC: Congressional Quarterly.

Putnam, R. D. (1996, January 10). Why we're on our worst behavior. *Chicago Tribune,* sec. 1, p. 17.

Renshon, S. A. (1996). *The psychological assessment of the president.* New York: New York University Press.

Rubel, C. (1995, August). TV still powerful, but Web sites offer new stump for pols. *Marketing News,* pp. 5-6.

Shalt, R. (1997, July 1). Dr. Spin: It's all in the lighting. *Gentleman's Quarterly,* p. 19.

Sheppard, N., Jr. (1995, December 12). Hate groups embrace cyberspace as weapon. *Chicago Tribune,* sec. 1, pp. 1, 23.

Simon, P. (1995, November 26). Mr. Simon returns from Washington. *Chicago Tribune,* sec. 2, pp. 1, 9.

Simon, R. (1998, December 19). With "approval and pride," Mrs. Clinton defends her husband. *Chicago Tribune,* sec. 1, p. 1.

Slocum, W. (1996, April). Voter services in cyberspace. *Campaigns & Elections,* pp. 45-52.

Smith, R. (1997, Winter). Letting America speak. *Audacity,* pp. 50-62.

Smith, W. (1997, February 8). Defiant radio pirates tuning out FCC. *Chicago Tribune,* sec. 1, pp. 1, 11.

Souza, P. (1998, April 5). Decisive moments are few when you must capture history on cue. *Chicago Tribune* (Perspective), pp. 1, 10.

Stevenson, S. (1998, January 22). Invisible ink: How the story everyone's talking about stayed out of the papers. *Slate: Tangled Web.*

Tackett, M. (1995a, May 25). Candidates go on-line to net votes. *Chicago Tribune,* sec. 1, pp. 1, 22.

Tackett, M. (1995b, February 23). '96 money game: More early primaries put premium on big political war chests. *Chicago Tribune,* sec. 1, p. 14.

Tackett, M. (1996, August 9). Right-wing rules on GOP platform. *Chicago Tribune,* sec. 1, pp. 1, 24.

Tackett, M. (1997, January 17). Outgoing GOP chief issues warning. *Chicago Tribune,* sec. 1, p. 3.

Tackett, M. (1998, June 19). A record low turnout possible in November. *Chicago Tribune,* sec. 1, p. 6.

Tech report. (1998, January 23). *USA Today.*

Terris, M., & Jaye, E. (1995, September). The art of the self-mailer: How to grab attention step-by-step. *Campaigns & Elections,* pp. 34-35.

The War Room. Documentary film on the 1992 Clinton presidential campaign.

Thurber, J. A., & Nelson, C. J. (Eds.). (1995). *Campaigns and elections American style.* Boulder, CO: Westview.

Ullmann, O. (1995, May 22). Maybe even the general can't outflank the two-party system. *Business Week,* pp. 57-58.

Van, J. (1997, April 27). Telecommuter Congress. *Chicago Tribune,* sec. 2, pp. 1, 4.

Warren, J. (1995, May 14). No more shades of gray. *Chicago Tribune,* sec. 5, p. 2.

Warren, J. (1997, December 3). The campaign merry-go-round requires ever-deeper pockets. *Chicago Tribune,* sec. 1, pp. 1, 28.

White, T. (1961). *The making of the president.* New York. Atheneum House.

Woodward, B. (1994). *The agenda: Inside the Clinton White House.* New York: Simon & Schuster.

Wright, R. (1995, January 23). Hyper democracy. *Time,* p. 18.

Zorn, E. (1995, December 14). Internet freedom calls up worries of a bygone era. *Chicago Tribune,* sec. 2, p. 1.

Additional Reading

Egan, J. J. (1995, August 27). Time to practice the "L" word again? *Chicago Tribune,* sec. 4, p. 3.

Garland, S. B., & Dunham, R. S. (1993, February 22). Polling for policy. *Business Week,* pp. 34-35.

Kelly, M. (1992, November 12). The making of a first family: A blueprint. *New York Times,* sec. 1, p. 9.

Klein, J. (1993, June 7). What's wrong? *Newsweek,* pp. 16-19.

Kramer, M. (1995, September 15). Just like Ike. *Time,* pp. 73-74.

Neikirk, W. (1994, August 23). Clinton's cliffhangers chip away at his image. *Chicago Tribune,* sec. 1, pp. 1, 11.

Newman, B. I. (1992, June). Gulf and Bush / Bush and Gulf: U.S. pre- and post-war propaganda—One year later. *Werbeforschung & Praxis,* pp. 3-9.

Newman, B. I. (1994, February). The forces behind the merging of marketing and politics. *Werbeforschung & Praxis,* pp. 41-47.

Newman, B. I., & Sheth, J. N. (1985). *Political marketing: Readings and annotated bibliography.* Chicago: American Marketing Association.

Newman, B. I., & Sheth, J. N. (1987). *A theory of political choice behavior.* New York: Praeger.

Schmuhl, R. (1994, January 20). 1993: Clinton's roller-coaster year. *Chicago Tribune,* sec. 1, p. 21.

Seib, G. F., & Stout, H. (1997, January 20). Clinton plans to turn to the political center if he can find it. *Wall Street Journal,* pp. A1, A11.

Stanton, W. J. (1971). *Fundamentals of marketing.* New York: McGraw-Hill.

Tackett, M. (1998, September 17). Televised images can cast unflattering light. *Chicago Tribune,* p. 21.

Van, J. (1996, January 8). Cybercafes serving a blend with byte. *Chicago Tribune,* sec. 1, pp. 1, 12.

Worthington, R. (1997, January 12). ONTHERECORD. *Chicago Tribune,* sec. 2, p. 3.

Name Index

Subject Index

About the Author

Bruce I. Newman is nationally and internationally known as one of the leading authorities on the subject of political marketing. He has authored or edited five books on the subject of politics and marketing including *The Marketing of the President* (1994) and *Handbook of Political Marketing* (1999). He also has co-authored two books on the subject of consumer psychology, *Consumption Values and Market Choices* (1991) and *Customer Behavior* (1998). He served as an adviser to senior aides in the Clinton White House on communication strategy for the 1996 presidential election.

Newman is an associate professor in the marketing department in the Kellstadt Graduate School of Business at DePaul University. Prior to that, he was on the faculties of Baruch College, City University of New York, and the University of Wisconsin–Milwaukee. He also was a visiting professor at Trinity College in Dublin, Ireland, and a visiting scholar at FMD Research Institute in Oslo, Norway. He received his B.S., M.B.A., and Ph.D. (1981) degrees in marketing from the University of Illinois in Champaign-Urbana. He currently sits on the editorial boards of *Psychology and Marketing* and *Werbeforschung & Praxis.*

Newman lectures around the world on the subjects of political marketing and voting behavior and is a frequent contributor to the mass media. He is a frequent guest on television talk shows and has been quoted in numerous national newspapers, with op-ed articles appearing in the *Christian Science Monitor,* the *Chicago Tribune,* and the *Sunday Telegraph.* In 1993, he received the Ehrenring (Ring of Honor) from the Austrian Advertising Research Association in Vienna for his research in political marketing. He is the first American recipient of this award in the 30 years it has been given out.